"This fun and engaging book includes  designed to change the thoughts and fectionism alive. The strategies in th are rooted in cognitive behavioral researched, effective approach for dea perfectionism. If perfectionism is a problem for you or someone you care about, I highly recommend checking out *The Monkey Mind Workout for Perfectionism*."

—**Martin M. Antony, PhD, ABPP,**
professor of psychology at Ryerson University in Toronto, ON, Canada; and coauthor of *When Perfect Isn't Good Enough* and *The Shyness and Social Anxiety Workbook*

"Jennifer Shannon is back with thirty exercises to tame your inner perfectionist! From setting realistic goals and expectations to jump-starting those tasks you dread, she offers specific, concrete exercises with which you can compassionately rein in those habits of compulsive perfectionism."

—**Dave Carbonell, PhD**, "coach" at www.anxietycoach.com; and author of *Panic Attacks Workbook, The Worry Trick,* and *Fear of Flying Workbook*

"If you think that your perfectionism is ingrained in your personality and you just have to live with it, then here's some great news: *The Monkey Mind Workout for Perfectionism* will change your mind-set by asking you to make small and deliberate changes in your actions. Enough with setting such sky-high standards that you are doomed to failure. Enough of all those disappointments and self-criticism. Jennifer Shannon has been there and done that. Let her book liberate you from the tyranny of perfect. When you finish this workout, you'll get to unleash your creativity, your purpose, and your self-compassion."

—**Reid Wilson, PhD**, author of
Stopping the Noise in Your Head

"Jennifer Shannon understands perfectionism inside out! Her engaging explanations and creative exercises are expertly designed and paced. Perfectionists are in good hands as she coaches us through daily exercises to help us learn to accept, and even enjoy, a less than perfect life."

—**Christine A. Padesky, PhD**, coauthor of
Mind Over Mood

"Jennifer Shannon has written another nearly perfect book. In *The Monkey Mind Workout for Perfectionism*, she describes the illusion that perfectionism promises and the soul-crushing reality that it delivers. Take heart, though. Jennifer presents a path forward, filled with compassion, insight, and a host of activities that will calm any perfectionist's 'monkey mind.' I highly recommend it."

—**Michael A. Tompkins, PhD, ABPP,**
codirector of the San Francisco Bay Area Center for Cognitive Therapy; assistant clinical professor at the University of California, Berkeley; and author of *The Anxiety and Depression Workbook*

THE
MONKEY
MiND
WORKOUT FOR

PERFECTIONISM

BREAK FREE *from* **ANXIETY &**
BUILD SELF-COMPASSION *in* **30 DAYS!**

JENNIFER SHANNON, LMFT
Illustrations by **DOUG SHANNON**

New Harbinger Publications, Inc.

NEW HARBINGER PUBLICATIONS is a registered trademark of New Harbinger Publications, Inc.

Distributed in Canada by Raincoast Books

Copyright © 2021 by Jennifer Shannon
New Harbinger Publications, Inc.
5674 Shattuck Avenue
Oakland, CA 94609
www.newharbinger.com

Illustrations by Doug Shannon

Cover design by Amy Shoup; Acquired by Tesilya Hanauer; Edited by James Lainsbury

Library of Congress Cataloging-in-Publication Data

Names: Shannon, Jennifer, author.
Title: The monkey mind workout for perfectionism : break free from anxiety and build self-compassion in 30 days! / Jennifer Shannon.
Description: Oakland, CA : New Harbinger Publications, [2021]
Identifiers: LCCN 2021003067 | ISBN 9781684037216 (trade paperback)
Subjects: LCSH: Perfectionism (Personality trait) | Anxiety--Treatment. | Self-acceptance.
Classification: LCC BF698.35.P47 S53 2021 | DDC 155.2/32--dc23
LC record available at https://lccn.loc.gov/2021003067

Printed in the United States of America

23   22   21

10   9   8   7   6   5   4   3   2   1   First Printing

Contents

The Workout

Introduction

Despite all the scrutiny it has received in the last two decades, perfectionism still holds a romantic allure for us. In our competitive culture, performance and presentation are closely associated with power, success, and higher social status. But the cost of our enchantment is high. If we dare not risk making a mistake or misstep, and cannot forgive ourselves when we do, we deny ourselves the freedom to risk, to create, to explore, and to fully engage with the flow of life. Ultimately, our inability to forgive our own fallibility continues to be the single biggest obstacle to our professional success, our relationships, and our own personal growth and happiness.

Readers of my previous book, *Don't Feed the Monkey Mind*, will recognize perfectionist thinking as one of the three pillars—alongside being overly responsible and intolerant of uncertainty—of what I call the *monkey mind-set*, the reactive way we think when we're hijacked by the fight-or-flight alarms of our brain's limbic system, which we experience as fear and anxiety. To think that we should, or even can, be consistently perfect is a false assumption, and the wisdom of accepting our imperfect selves unconditionally is self-evident. Yet we continue to beat ourselves up for every perceived failure and shortcoming. Why?

As you'll discover in this book, perfectionism is not only a pattern of thinking, it is a pattern of behavior. As a cognitive behavioral therapist, I work not just with the cognitions, or thoughts, of my clients, but with their behavior as well. These clients have proven to me time and time again that for any new way of thinking to take root, it must be harnessed to a new way of *doing.* That is why this book—the first of three, each addressing one pillar of the monkey mind-set—is a *workout* book. To benefit, you'll not only need to break your perfectionist pattern of thinking, you'll need to break your perfectionist pattern of behavior as well. In other words, you'll have to break a sweat! With each exercise, you'll develop more of the resilience and confidence you need to free yourself from the tyranny of perfect, enabling you to truly *believe* that you are enough as you are.

Before you begin, take my Perfectionism Quiz, available for download at http://monkeymindbooks.com/p/. The quiz will help you evaluate to what extent perfectionism is affecting your life.

The Little Perfectionist

"Class, I have a special announcement. Someone in our class has won the school essay contest!" My fifth-grade teacher was beaming. Her eyes scanned our faces, building our anticipation. I felt a burst of hope in my chest, like the first kernel of popcorn popping in the pot. *But it can't be me,* said the little voice in my head. *My essay is lousy!*

The subject of my "lousy" essay was Patrick Henry, the founding father who said, "Give me liberty or give me death," and I'd suffered a thousand deaths writing it. For the past two weeks, every day after school, I had shuttered myself in my room for hours, writing and rejecting what I'd written until the floor was littered with crumpled paper. When my mother tried to help, I took each suggestion as criticism, confirmation that I wasn't up to the task. Many writing sessions ended with me in tears. On the last night, I cobbled together a single-page, double-spaced essay to hand in. And now, to my amazement, my teacher's adoring gaze was fixed on me!

"Congratulations, Jenny," she said. I felt my heart fill with pride. "Come up here and read your winning essay to the class." She held out her arm, beckoning me to the front of the room.

What? My heart beat with fear. Reading something aloud in class had always made me anxious, but *These are* my words! *I thought.* Everyone will hear out loud how poorly I write. And what if I mispronounce something? I'll look stupid. *I slunk down in my seat, trying to disappear. After some futile attempts to persuade me, my teacher read the essay to the class herself. Listening to it was excruciating; every word sounded stupid and false. When she finished, I breathed a big sigh of relief.*

Poor little me! I'd worked myself into a state of emotional exhaustion trying to write an essay good enough for my teacher and classmates. At the tender age of eleven, I was already a full-blown perfectionist. Imagine my horror when I found out that winning my local elementary school's contest meant I had to write a *new* essay for the district-level contest!

Now, half a century later, I'm a therapist specializing in anxiety disorders. Before I begin working with new clients, I ask them what their therapy goals are. The most common answer is, "I want to feel less anxious and better about myself."

Whether you've ever considered therapy, you've been to therapy, or you're a therapist like me, this goal is easy to relate to. If we didn't feel so anxious and liked ourselves more, we could be more spontaneous and authentic around others, not overly concerned with how they might judge or criticize us. Instead of agonizing over what we should do all the time, we could follow the desires of our heart. We could take bigger risks, get creative, and then forgive ourselves whenever we fall short. And when we got tired, instead of pushing on until we dropped, we'd stop and take care of ourselves, even if our work wasn't done. We wouldn't have to fake believing in ourselves; we'd be genuinely self-confident.

For perfectionists like us, there is a formidable obstacle to achieving genuine self-confidence. Like little Jenny writing her essay, in any venture we undertake we must face our biggest critic: ourselves.

Broken Bubbles, Values Lost

How many times have we vowed to be kinder to ourselves? To talk to ourselves as we would a good friend who is suffering? We earnestly recite positive affirmations that we are lovable, worthy, and deserving of respect. We promise to stop comparing ourselves to supermodels, athletes, and start-up entrepreneurs. In countless inspirational books, seminars, dharma talks, and TED Talks, we've been told, "You are enough," and we *so* want to believe it. We vow that, from this day forward, we will love ourselves more despite our imperfections. Self-acceptance and compassion will be the final solution, the antidote to our dis-ease!

Then reality hits. Walking out of a morning meeting you realize that you left out an important talking point. You think, *How could I have made such a stupid mistake?* At noon, you're hungry and tired and need a break, but *I can't stop until this report is done!* You've been told to delegate more, but *If my coworkers mess up, it will reflect poorly on me.* You leave work late, feeling stressed and irritable.

At home you pick up the mail and notice an overdue bill. *Why do I put bills off? Why can't I just pay them when they arrive?* You change into your jeans and they feel tight. *I'm ugly and fat!* At the park with your kids, you snap at your youngest for wanting to go to the restroom for the third time. *I'm a lousy parent!* Your partner complains that you didn't take the garbage out, and you practically bite their head off. *Where's the gratitude for what I did do?*

That evening you see posts of your friends having an amazing European vacation. *Why don't I have enough money to take nice vacations like that?* And just as you're turning out the light, a reminder pops up on your phone. *I forgot an item on my to-do list!* Now you're feeling just plain crappy about yourself. Then you remember your promise to be accepting of and compassionate toward yourself. You tell yourself, *I'm okay just the way I am.*

But it's stale and unconvincing. You can't even do self-compassion properly! You think, *It would be a lot easier to believe that I'm good enough if I were just a little bit better!*

Of course, for perfectionists, "a little bit better" would hardly be enough. For us, self-acceptance and compassion are always conditional. We think, *I am only worthy if I get everything done correctly, if I impress my boss, if I*

lose some weight, if…the list goes on and on. For perfectionists, life is an endless series of mistakes to be avoided and abilities to be proven, and when we fail, we must be punished. For our positive affirmation bubbles to last, they must withstand not only the jagged edges of our lives, but the pointed jabs of our own self-judgments.

To make matters more confusing for the perfectionist, performing perfectly, and avoiding whatever we cannot perform perfectly, can look like a winning—that is, "perfect"—strategy. With blood, sweat, and tears, and a little luck, we often win promotions at work, get to manage others and be better paid, and impress our community and secure higher social status. But look at the price we pay for our *perfectionism.*

When we can't abide criticism, we will not be open to feedback that might help us grow.

When we can't tolerate mistakes, we can't commit to things that take trial and error to master.

When we can't stop working until everything is done, and done well, we can't stop for self-care or quality time with our family and friends.

When we are afraid of others judging us, we can't be honest, authentic, and vulnerable.

When we are afraid of failure, we will not have the courage to pursue the difficult goals that will bring us the greatest fulfillment in life.

When we need everything to be done "our way," we will not be able to delegate tasks and get help from others.

In our pursuit to be perfect, we sacrifice the values of spontaneity, creativity, authenticity, self-care, connection, purpose, and self-compassion. We can survive without them, but can we thrive? The prevalence of anxiety, depression, and burnout in our society is strong evidence that many of us are merely surviving. It's no wonder that self-medicating with drugs and alcohol, soothing ourselves with comfort food, and distracting ourselves with shopping and social media are the norm rather than the exceptions.

When we know the price we're paying for our perfectionism, we might ask, why is it so difficult to relax our grip on ourselves? Why can't we just decide to be more easygoing? Does letting go of perfect really have to be a *workout*? Yes, because the moment we make allowances for mistakes or failures in our lives, we must reckon with a fiercely oppositional force within: our primordial drive for survival.

Feeding the Monkey

Staying alive has always been job number one for us—we can't be confident and creative or spontaneously joyful if we're dead. As a species, we've performed wonderfully in this capacity, despite our lack of fur to protect us from the elements, or claws or sharp teeth to ward off predators. We generally credit our highly evolved frontal lobe for this success, but we must also thank the oldest part of our brain, the *limbic system,* a cluster of gray matter located at the base of our skull. It's hardwired for our survival, humming along in the background, monitoring everything we're experiencing—what we see, hear, feel, and think—for threats to our safety and well-being. It acts as an early warning system, sounding *fight-or-flight* alarms long before we're conscious of any danger.

For the perfectionist, the limbic system is particularly sensitive to the threat of making a mistake, which indicates weakness that could draw criticism from others and threaten our social status. Due to our genetic temperament or life experience, or both, the limbic system triggers alarms—neurochemicals and hormones that we experience as negative emotions—at inappropriate times. If the noodles are overcooked, we feel angry at ourselves. *How could I have messed this up?* If someone's looking at their cell phone during our presentation, we feel panic. *Am I boring everybody?* If somebody works out harder in the gym than we do, drives a nicer car, or has kids who get better grades than ours, we feel inadequate and ashamed. *Do I have everyone's respect?*

The oversensitivity of our limbic system is why we can't let up on ourselves for a second, why we like to be in control, why everything has to be "just so." For us, failure is not an option. If we can't do it right, we shouldn't do it at all. *Any* possibility of being criticized or rejected by those we depend on—whether it's our bosses, coworkers, family, or friends—feels like an existential threat. Our primordial fear of being rejected, alone, and vulnerable in a dangerous world prevails.

For some, perfectionism is a fair price to pay for survival. But as we know, staying alive, while an important thing, isn't the *only* thing. Living in denial of our own human fallibility, without allowance or compassion for our own mistakes and shortcomings, isn't really living. If only we could dial down our limbic system a bit, so we could get less fight-or-flight and more *rest-and-digest*, we could be a little more compassionate with ourselves, a little more easygoing.

But this part of the brain is independent, with a mind of its own. It doesn't honor our personal values, or any value other than survival. It hijacks the rest of our brain—highly evolved frontal lobe and all—into thinking we can't let up, even when we're burned out. When our limbic system becomes our master, instead of our servant, what can we do?

The first, and most important, thing we can do is gain some psychological distance from our limbic system. It isn't us, only a part of us—a brain-within-a-brain, firewalled away from our direct control. With its lightning-quick reactivity, inability to reason or assess risk, and aggressive determination to prevent us from getting kicked out of our tribe, it has an animal character all its own. That's why I like to call it the "monkey mind." *Woo-woo-woo! Make no mistakes!* is the law of the jungle of our unconscious.

Fortunately, we are conscious beings who can train ourselves to override our unconscious drive for "perfect." And when we train ourselves to accept imperfection, we train the monkey mind to be less reactive to it.

The Cycle of Perfectionism

Let's return to my Patrick Henry essay story and look at my experience from the perspective of the monkey mind. The idea that I might fail to impress my teacher and classmates and be criticized, even though it was only a possibility, was, to my dialed-up limbic system, a serious threat. To alert me to what it perceived as an unacceptable risk, I received a dose of fight-or-flight feelings, the monkey's call to action: *Woo-woo-woo! Do something about this!*

I answered the call by sequestering myself in my room to write. If I was uncertain whether what I was writing was good enough, I crumpled the paper and started over. I drove myself to the point of exhaustion trying to secure everyone's approval.

My behavior was part of a chain reaction. The *thought* that I might not meet my tribe's expectations was, from the perspective of the monkey mind, a threat, which triggered an alarm, a *feeling* of anxiety, which prompted my *reaction*—overthinking and overworking.

Thought-feeling-reaction chains happen in our lives hundreds of times a day. Some are as dramatic as my essay example, but most we're barely conscious of. When we do notice these chain reactions, we tend to see them as isolated incidents. Once we learn to recognize them, however, we can see that each thought-feeling-reaction chain is really just one section of a much longer chain. Let's look at how one thought-feeling-reaction chain leads to another.

With our survival always at stake, the monkey mind is monitoring *everything* closely, including how we answer its call to action. When I reacted to my anxiety by working harder—trying to get rid of the feeling—I sent the monkey a message of my own. I confirmed its perception that I was under threat. When our reactions tell our limbic system that it's doing a good job, we're programming it to make more false alarms and to deliver more anxiety in similar situations in the future. For the perfectionist, responding to anxiety about being criticized or judged is the banana that feeds the monkey, fueling a cycle of anxiety about being criticized or judged.

Woo-woo-woo!

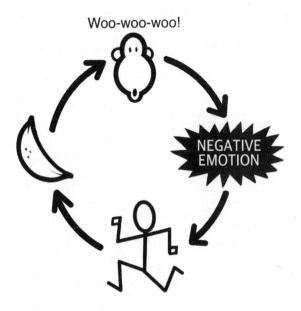

For the perfectionist, avoiding mistakes and staying in control strengthens our conviction that we must do so, and vice versa. As in all of life, what goes around comes around.

Beliefs and Behaviors

The symbiotic relationship between our beliefs and our behaviors is beautifully illustrated in the following joke.

> A longtime resident of New York City was giving a visitor a guided tour of Manhattan. As they were crossing Fifth Avenue, the New Yorker suddenly leaped into the air, landing on a manhole cover with a clanging thud. For the next several blocks, at every manhole he repeated this behavior.
>
> "What in the world are you doing?" the baffled tourist finally asked.
>
> "I'm scaring the alligators to keep them from crawling out of the sewers," his guide replied.
>
> "That's absurd," scoffed the tourist, "the most absurd thing I've ever heard!"
>
> "Look around," replied his guide. "Do you see any alligators?"
>
> "No," the visitor admitted.
>
> "Then it may be absurd," said the proud New Yorker, "but it works!"

As any first-year student of statistics will tell you, correlation does not equal causation. A random behavior like jumping on manhole covers may precede a positive outcome, such as "no visible alligators," but it is hardly the cause. Saying, "*Because I jumped on the manhole covers, there are no alligators here,*" is, as the visitor to New York observes, absurd.

But we make equally absurd, unconscious correlations all the time. Remember when I refused to read my essay aloud to the class? Nobody had the chance to laugh at me reading it. Seeing the outcome of my behavior, the monkey mind concluded, *Because I stopped you from reading aloud to the class, you maintained the respect of your classmates and are safe.* Similarly, when I won the contest, despite the many fruitless hours of self-doubt and wasted effort, the monkey concluded, *Because I compelled you to work harder, you are safe and in the good graces of your teacher.* We might call these simplistic, even absurd, conclusions *monkey logic,* a rationale that judges outcomes solely on how safe we are from criticism, judgment, or rejection.

Perfectionist Beliefs

Because monkey logic is woven so tightly into the fabric of our unconscious, we can't see the pattern it creates. Do any of these statements sound familiar to you?

Mistakes, judgments, and criticisms from others mean that I'm not good enough.

I should only feel good about myself if I've done something well.

I can't depend on others because they won't do things the way they should be done.

If anyone is better than I am at something, then I'm not good enough.

If I fail, it means I'm inferior.

If I can't do something perfectly, I shouldn't do it at all.

These perfectionist beliefs all have one important thing in common: they don't serve us; they serve the limbic system's survival agenda. When we feed the monkey with our perfectionist behaviors, we feed what becomes our own *monkey mindset*. This way of thinking allows for little self-acceptance or compassion when we err, discourages us from trusting others to do things right, and keeps us perpetually grasping for control.

Perfectionist Behaviors

Identifying perfectionist behavior can be difficult because so much of what we do qualifies as such. Taking on a heavy load at the office can look like a healthy display of our strengths and ambition, but if we're neglecting our health and loved ones, we might be overcompensating for our fear of failure. We think, *The more I accomplish, the less likely I am to be criticized.* Overworking is classic behavior of the overachieving perfectionist, and it's easy to rationalize because, along with burnout, overworking can bring short-term success.

Avoiding commitments and procrastinating, behaviors classified as "lazy," can be forms of perfectionism too. How? If our unconscious thought is, *If I don't take on this task, I won't fail at it and be criticized,* then it's driven by perfectionism. Whether we're over- or underachieving, or both, depending on the situation, if what we do is a reaction to the fear of failure and, ultimately, rejection, we're feeding the monkey.

Perfectionists receive microdoses of fight-or-flight neurochemicals—and react with perfectionist microbehaviors—dozens, even hundreds, of times a day. As you consider the following behaviors, ask yourself, *What threat to my survival am I confirming with this behavior?*

- Overpreparing for meetings to reduce the risk of making a mistake

- Denying myself sleep, recreation, and family time unless all my tasks are done—and done well

- Working overtime to make sure I stay ahead of everyone else

- Refusing to delegate tasks because other people don't meet my standards, which might reflect on me

- Putting off tasks until there is so little time left to complete them that I can safely lower my expectations

- Refusing to ask questions, thinking they will reveal my ignorance

- Trying to mask my anxiety and lower my inhibitions with drugs or alcohol in social situations

- Avoiding people, places, and activities that make me anxious

- Refusing to try things that I haven't mastered

- Hiding my own deficiency or ignorance to protect my own sense of competency

When examining perfectionist behavior, we must also consider the behavior in our heads whenever we make a mistake or fall short of our expectations: judging and criticizing *ourselves*. Like the outwardly observable behaviors on the list above, trashing ourselves is a reaction to uncomfortable emotions. We think being shamed will incentivize us to drive ourselves harder, preventing future failures. While that kind of motivational tactic may bring some short-term success or status, it is guaranteed to burn us out.

All perfectionist behaviors are reactions to our limbic system, and, as such, they are motivated by negative emotion. To feel less anxious and better about ourselves, we need to stop taking orders from the most primitive part of our brain. We need to stop thinking with a monkey mind-set and teach the monkey who's boss.

Breaking the Cycle

Nearly a half century after my fifth-grade essay, I'm standing in a hallway with nine other contestants, waiting my turn to deliver my original seven-minute speech to four hundred fellow Toastmasters. Blood is pounding in my ears. My limbs tremble, my palms are damp with sweat, and my chest feels like it's going to explode. The adrenaline and cortisol running through my veins are telling me to run for my life, that what I'm trying to do could be fatal.

Yet I am in control. This was exactly what I planned and practiced for. I expected to feel terrified. I remind myself, These feelings are normal for this situation. They don't signify that anything is wrong. *I open myself up to these sensations, welcoming even my pounding heart and sweating armpits. I remember that my objective isn't to impress anyone or to win, but to share my personal message with others.* If I make a mistake, or embarrass myself in any way, it means I have taken a risk. Being willing to take this risk is how I define winning!

As the seconds tick by and my moment approaches, my sensations feel less like fear and more like another emotion: excitement. Passing a mirrored surface, I see that there's a smile on my face. As I step onto the stage into the glare of the spotlight and look out on a sea of expectant faces, instead of shrinking and wanting to disappear, I get bigger,

*as if I can encompass all my fear, as well as all the
expectations in the room. And as I give my speech,
tempering the physical sensations of terror, there is a joyful
sense of victory. With every word, every gesture I deliver
to the crowd, I am beating my most formidable opponent
in the contest, my monkey mind.*

I'm not telling you this story to illustrate what a great public speaker I am. I didn't win the competition, or even place. I'm sharing this experience because it demonstrates the three fundamental skills required to break the cycle of perfectionism, skills you'll be practicing while doing the exercises in this book.

The first is recognizing your monkey mind-set, with its narrow survival agenda and unrealistic expectations, and then redirecting yourself toward a more expansive mind-set that reflects your values. This skill resembles the affirmations we've all tried, except you won't be practicing in a nice safe bubble. The exercises in this book offer real-world experience. And instead of making vows or promises to stick with your new expansive way of thinking, you'll treat it as a new, expansive mind-set to keep returning to again and again. For example, on the morning of my speech, I repeatedly reminded myself that my fear was normal for the situation, and that by being willing to expose myself to everyone's judgment, I'd already won the most important contest that day.

The second skill is replacing your perfectionist behaviors with behaviors that reflect your higher personal values. You'll do this with ordinary day-to-day situations. (Don't worry, I won't ask you to compete on stage!) Each new behavior will create a new experience that gives you a taste of what freedom from perfectionism feels like. There is no substitute for this. We can't begin to believe we are enough until we begin to experience it.

The third skill is learning to *physically* tolerate negative emotions like embarrassment, shame, and fear of failure. To help you achieve this, these exercises will be done in relatively safe and low-stake situations that will trigger a *manageable* amount of anxiety. You'll know that the anxiety is only noisy monkey chatter, not a reliable signal that you're in danger, and you'll prepare yourself so you don't get blindsided by emotions. You'll learn firsthand that the better you get at tolerating uncomfortable emotions, the more quickly they play out and make room for excitement, passion, and even joy. You're going to get good at feeling bad!

Sound scary? That's understandable. Most of us have been doing everything possible to avoid negative emotions all our lives. How to tolerate negative emotions is also where most therapists and self-help books leave us hanging. Nobody wants to talk about accepting pain of any kind; that's painful to even think about!

Over my years as a therapist, I've heard from many clients, "My emotions are too great. They will overwhelm me, and I can't let that happen." It's a natural argument to make, and I've used it myself in the past. It's true that accepting anxiety, shame, fear, and other disruptive emotions is nearly impossible when we're blindsided by them—it's about as easy as accepting your shower running out of hot water before you've had a chance to rinse, or another driver cutting you off in traffic. But when we approach a situation knowing that our limbic system is just doing its job, with the *expectation* that we'll have uncomfortable emotions, we take away the monkey's big advantage of speed. Rather than reacting in surprise, we can respond wisely.

The Welcoming Breath

Have you ever dipped your toe in a pool and leaped back from the cold? Recoiling from chilly water is a reflex, our natural reaction to the fight-or-flight alarms of our limbic system warning us of potential danger. Should we decide that the joys of playing in the water are worth some discomfort, and we put our toe back in, we come up against a hard truth: we cannot acclimate to cold water without also acclimating to the fight-or-flight alarms of our limbic system, which is so devoted to our safety that a drop in temperature of even a few degrees in our surroundings is cause for alarm. *Woo-woo-woo!* the monkey chatters. *Something is wrong!*

Fists clenched, shoulders hunched, and holding our breath, we inch ourselves into the water. As we cringe and contort ourselves in an attempt to block out all sensation, we are unaware that we're sending a message to the monkey mind, which is watching us all the time. That message is, *I shouldn't have to feel this way! Something's wrong, and I can't handle it. Keep sounding the alarm!*

Each exercise in this workout will be like going for a swim in a cold pool. You'll know in advance to expect a *Woo-woo-woo!* from the monkey mind—feelings and sensations you are not going to like. You'll want to climb back out of the water and dry off in the sun. This behavior, as you are beginning to understand by now, has sustained your perfectionism. To reclaim your lost values, which in our pool metaphor would be the joy of playing in the water, you must acclimate to fight-or-flight feelings long enough for them to metabolize on their own. Otherwise, as you've likely discovered, they keep returning in situation after situation.

To allow fight-or-flight emotions to move through us efficiently—and quickly—we must counterintuitively embrace them and make space for them to play themselves out. We create and sustain that space by bringing our attention to the interior of our body through our breathing. With each intake of breath we invite the feelings in. With each out-breath we let go of trying to control them, allowing them to metabolize on their own. Because we are integrating our emotions rather than trying to override or neutralize them, I call this deceptively powerful tool the *welcoming breath*.

To help you get a handle on your own welcoming breath, try this little experiment.

Take a few moments to recall a mistake or failing in your past. How does this memory make you feel? Is it located anywhere specific? Or is it generalized throughout your body? Once you've identified and located the feeling as best you can, make two fists, clench your belly, and hunch your shoulders forward. Hold this position, and the memory, breathing as little as possible, for a count of thirty.

When you reach thirty, relax and sit up straight. How comfortable are you? Rate how your body feels on a scale of 1 to 10, with 1 being "Ugh!" and 10 being "Great!"

Now do the same exercise, first opening your hands and resting them palms up where you can see them. Lift the base of your head and pull your shoulder blades together. Focus your awareness on the interior of your body, breathing slowly and deeply into your chest and belly, following the air as it comes in and goes out. Continue to breathe in this manner while reimagining your failing or mistake for a count of thirty.

How comfortable are you this time? Rate how your body feels again on a scale of 1 to 10.

Contracting your body and breath, trying to suppress emotions in the exaggerated way you did in the first half of the exercise, was extreme. But we do this, to one degree or another, so often throughout our day that we don't question it. And while it can give us some sense of control, that control is short-lived at best, because it sends the wrong message to our limbic system. Our resistance to our feelings confirms that we shouldn't have to feel this way, that whatever triggered them is wrong, potentially a threat we can't handle. It feeds the monkey, training it to deliver more fight-or-flight emotions, both in the moment and in similar situations in the future.

Conversely, when we consciously welcome uncomfortable feelings, we're telling the monkey mind that we can handle them, that the idea or situation that provoked them is not a threat, and that there is no need for further alarm. The welcoming breath is the most powerful way to reclaim our mind and body when they're hijacked by the monkey. Breathing slowly, deeply, and deliberately soothes the limbic system, telling it to settle down. It is a beautiful paradox that welcoming discomfort in the moment is the way to get less of it in the future!

How to Do the Workout

There are thirty exercises in this workout, a month's worth in all, but you can do them in any order. Skip around as you see fit, and don't hesitate to repeat them. Each exercise is designed with plenty of room for personal adjustment, so feel free to tweak the instructions to fit you. If any exercise feels too difficult, just dial it back to your level of tolerance, or skip it for now and circle back later. And if an exercise sounds too easy, I suggest you do it anyway, just for fun. You might be surprised at what challenges arise. Either way, the more exercises you do, the more you will benefit from them.

Remember that the perfectionist mind-set colors every thought we have and action we take, right down to choosing what shoes to wear to work today. This means that *any* exercise you undertake in this workout will create a new experience that chips away at your perfectionist monkey mind-set.

Before you dive in, I'd like to break down the exercise format and decode the icons you'll see. Each exercise has an introductory page consisting of a short anecdote or an illustration, or both, as well as a question for you to think about. If possible, read this page the day before you do the exercise to give yourself time to warm to the challenge.

Each exercise begins with a muscle icon and a short description of what you're invited to do. Then follows a sequence of icons dividing the instructions into sections:

A brief explanation of the specific monkey mind-set that pertains to this exercise

 The expansive mind-set you'll be cultivating and the lost values you'll be reclaiming with the exercise

 The negative emotions that you'll welcome and allow to metabolize on their own

 A post-exercise review to help encourage praise and self-compassion

When I'm working with clients, I coach them through these exercises like a personal trainer would at a gym. I can't be your personal trainer here, but I've put together some online tools to help you coach yourself. At http://monkeymindbooks. com/p/, you'll find "workout sheets" that you can download and, for some exercises, guided meditations that you can stream, both of which will deepen your learning experience. You can also look for the icons that will appear at the start of each exercise to know what tools are available for it: the 🔊 icon denotes a workout sheet, while the ✎ icon denotes a guided meditation.

What is also missing in a book is the personal trainer voice cheering, "You are awesome. Keep it up!" Fortunately, praise doesn't have to come from someone else to be effective. You can pat yourself on the back, take a deep breath, or mouth the words "well done" to yourself. I also recommend a form of praise called *kinesthetic reinforcement,* a physical action that celebrates the new behavior you undertake. This action can be anything you choose—for example, moving a coin from one pocket to another. My personal favorite kinesthetic reinforcement is done with a simple accessory I call the *self-compassion band.*

Everybody has a drawer with rubber bands in it, so dig out a nice big one and slide it around your wrist. (If you have a stretchy beaded band or something similar, that's even better.) Each time you change a perfectionist behavior, welcome a negative emotion, or redirect yourself to your expansive mind-set, move the flexible band from one wrist to the other.

This simple ritual acts as a kinesthetic reinforcement for your workout, reminding you that what you did was difficult and that you deserve compassion. It's a way to praise yourself for the risks you took and the feelings you welcomed rather than resisted. Once you get an understanding of what behaviors and mind-sets you want to reinforce with self-compassion, you'll find plenty of opportunities throughout the day to utilize your self-compassion band. Some days I switch mine back and forth a dozen times.

Our Daily Sweat

I hope you'll commit to this workout for a full thirty days; however, I have bigger plans for you. From confronting my own perfectionism, I know that my journey will never end. The more I've worked on my perfectionist mind-set, the more aware I am of how subtly embedded it is. This means I never lack for opportunities to employ new behaviors, exercise my expansive mind-set, and welcome the sensations and emotions that arise. I've discovered that there is simply no limit to how far these three skills can take us.

Just think about it for a minute. Once you begin to tap into the qualities you value—spontaneity, creativity, authenticity, and self-compassion—why would you want to stop? I encourage you to view these thirty exercises as a template for every month in the next year. Each day is a fresh opportunity to exercise the skills that will cultivate the joy you want in your life. In fact, each day is not only an opportunity, but an obligation. You wouldn't go to the gym for a month and expect yourself to stay in shape forever after. We need to work out every day to keep growing. We need to get our daily sweat!

Before you begin any exercises, take the Perfectionism Quiz that I mentioned in the introduction, downloadable at http:// monkeymindbooks.com/p/. Your results will form the baseline with which to compare your perfectionism after the four weeks of the workout. But if you do this workout faithfully, you won't need the quiz to assure yourself that you're changing; the difference in your life will be palpable. You will take better care of yourself than you ever have before. You will be empowered to make quicker and firmer decisions, knowing that your choice needn't—can't, in fact—be perfect. You'll find yourself willing to take bigger risks in your work and social life, leading to more creativity, confidence, and spontaneity—all values that are lost when you're stuck in perfectionism.

When those risks don't work out as hoped, or you make a mistake, you'll be much more forgiving of yourself, framing the experience as an opportunity to learn, not to be ashamed. And should you actually be criticized or rejected for anything you do, thanks to your welcoming breath and expanded mind-set, you'll be more resilient than ever. After all, once you've stood up to your biggest critic, your hijacked self, everyone else is easier to manage.

And, of course, the less you feed the monkey, the better regulated your limbic system will become—less geared toward *fight-or-flight* and more willing to help you *rest-and-digest*. This means more peace, more presence in each new moment, and more potential joy within. So, let's get started, shall we? Remember, the only bad exercise is the one that didn't happen.

Note: *Supplementary materials for the exercises can be accessed at* http://monkeymindbooks.com/p/.

The Workout

My client Johanna was excited about her upcoming trip to
see her mother, whom she had not visited for over a year.
"We had a falling-out," Johanna told me, and then went
on to describe how overbearing and opinionated her
mother was, and how she pushed her diametrically opposite
political views on Johanna, baiting her into endless debates.
When her mother started criticizing Johanna's parenting
of her two teenage children, Johanna decided she'd had
enough, and stopped communication with her. Her mother
reciprocated.

But Johanna felt differently now. Her new goal was
to heal this relationship, and during her upcoming visit she
wanted to keep an open, compassionate heart. Could I help
her accomplish this, she wanted to know. She was shocked
when I told her no.

While Johanna's was a noble goal, it wasn't realistic.
It was a perfectionist's expectation, one that didn't recognize
the inevitable human errors that happen when we are doing
something new and challenging. Keeping her heart open in
the face of her mother's judgments and aggression would be
akin to keeping the front door open in a hurricane. And
being compassionate to her mother would be difficult for
Johanna when she would be needing compassion for herself.

I told Johanna that I could *help her develop a more realistic expectation for herself. Although a bit disappointed, she agreed. Since we knew she would inevitably be triggered by something her mother would say or do, we decided that rather than expecting herself to "rise above," she should use a strategy to reduce tension. For example, when she felt herself getting angry, she could go to the bathroom and splash cold water on her face, or use humor in her response. Her overall goal was simply to keep opening her heart whenever possible, but not expecting it to remain open. At the end of each day, she could evaluate whether she met her realistic goal and praise herself if she did.*

Johanna met her realistic goal for the visit, and while her relationship with her mother was still testy, there were several moments of affection and understanding that they both recognized and appreciated. Johanna is already planning her next visit and is thinking about realistic goals for it, too.

Had Johanna attempted the visit with her unrealistic, perfectionistic goal, she would have failed. She would have returned home more resentful toward her mother for making it impossible to have an open, compassionate heart. And she would have been angry at herself for not being more loving. Only by setting realistic expectations can we engage our compassion for others, as well as for ourselves.

Are the expectations you place on yourself reasonable? The following foundational exercise will help you set goals that will enhance your experience and increase satisfaction, regardless of what you're doing or how imperfectly you're doing it.

1 Set a Reasonable Goal

Think of a task or an activity you have planned for today. Before you start it, (1) identify your unrealistic expectation about how you will do, and (2) replace it with a realistic goal. Afterward, (3) evaluate how you performed using that realistic goal. Whatever you're planning to do today, whether it's writing a report or meditating, conversing with others, cooking, or parenting, you'll likely be saddled with the unconscious expectation that you do it skillfully, without mistakes or setbacks. This exercise will help you allow for human fallibility and unpredictable circumstance, and experience the task or activity in a new way. Download the workout sheet for this exercise at http://monkeymindbooks .com/p/, and let's get started.

The monkey mind-set of *If I meet the highest standard, nobody can criticize me*, dictates that our report must be game changing and free of spelling and grammatical errors. Our meditation should be blissful with no intrusive thoughts. In conversation, we must be smart and funny and appear confident. Meals we cook should elicit compliments, and we must always be attuned, patient, and loving with our children, as well as our parents. Expectations like these turn our daily activities into an endless audition. If we let up on ourselves for a minute, we imagine we'll lose our motivation and start settling for mediocrity.

But it's hard to take any satisfaction from what we do when we're always falling short of our own expectations and punishing ourselves with shame. It's no wonder so many perfectionists suffer from poor self-esteem, anxiety, and stress. We feel like imposters in our own lives!

☀ While we may associate perfect performance with the winners in life, every biography ever written documents that the path to high achievement is fraught with bumps, pitfalls, and learning curves. Nobody in history traveled that path without tripping, falling, and taking wrong turns. To best achieve any goal in life, we want to adopt a mind-set that takes this reality into account: *Realistic goals will help me be a high achiever in life.* We won't be afraid to try new things and we will have the determination to keep going when we inevitably make mistakes. Instead of punishing ourselves, we can give ourselves much deserved encouragement for trying something new.

If you've expected unrealistic performances from yourself for a long time, it can be difficult to create realistic expectations. The basic rule is to dial it down. When writing a report, expect yourself only to communicate clearly without careless errors. When meditating, expect intrusive thoughts, and when you notice them, return your attention to your breath. In conversation, initiate eye contact regularly, practice listening, and speak truthfully. With the meal you cook, aim for edible.

Setting a realistic goal for yourself today is going to bring up some limbic resistance. You may have feelings of doubt and anxiety—that by lowering your standards you will pay the price of being judged by others. And since mistakes are inevitable, you're likely to feel ashamed at some point. All these emotions are normal and predictable alerts from the monkey mind that something is wrong, that you're not safe. Don't get hijacked. Use your welcoming breath, and remind yourself of your expansive mind-set. Unconditional self-acceptance is what you're after; it serves as the foundation for personal growth and high achievement. And to remind yourself of that, move your self-compassion band from one wrist to the other, then place your hand on your heart.

As with every exercise in this book, evaluating how well you met the goal of the exercise is essential, so don't skip this step. Did you keep reminding yourself of your realistic goal? Or did you slip back into unrealistic expectations? Did you welcome the emotions that arose, or did you try to fight them off? Give yourself a star for each success. And if you wound up blowing the task or not enjoying the activity because of your new approach, great! You get a bonus star for experiencing that!

Just as it takes many turns of the wheel to change the direction of an ocean liner, it will take many repetitions of this exercise before you'll come to believe that it's safe to drop unrealistic expectations from the tasks and activities in your life. From now on, look at everything you do as an opportunity to set a realistic goal. Every time you take the wheel you are correcting your course, adopting a way of doing that creates less stress, more learning, and greater satisfaction.

Do you hate leaving a job unfinished? Is it hard for you stop working on a task if it's not done? Tomorrow you'll discover the benefit of knowing when to quit.

Time That Task! 2

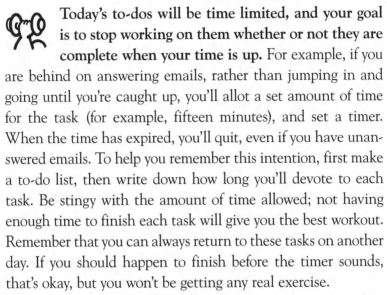

Today's to-dos will be time limited, and your goal is to stop working on them whether or not they are complete when your time is up. For example, if you are behind on answering emails, rather than jumping in and going until you're caught up, you'll allot a set amount of time for the task (for example, fifteen minutes), and set a timer. When the time has expired, you'll quit, even if you have unanswered emails. To help you remember this intention, first make a to-do list, then write down how long you'll devote to each task. Be stingy with the amount of time allowed; not having enough time to finish each task will give you the best workout. Remember that you can always return to these tasks on another day. If you should happen to finish before the timer sounds, that's okay, but you won't be getting any real exercise.

While you could do this exercise at your place of employment, it's probably best done on your day off, when you might have chores you want to get done. You can do the exercise with small tasks like watering plants or paying bills, or with bigger long-term tasks, like cleaning your garage or preparing a PowerPoint presentation for a meeting.

A squirrel doesn't stop gathering nuts to take the afternoon off in October. Its survival depends on having enough food to get through a cold, hard winter. As perfectionists, we have the same impulse. We keep cleaning our garage until it's organized, answering emails until our inbox is empty, or researching a question until we find the answer as if our survival depends on it. We are dancing to the jungle beat of the monkey mind: *I must finish what I start, or else I am lazy and vulnerable to threats!* Acting with this mind-set not only feeds the monkey, it can also hurt productivity. Tasks we don't think we can finish in one session get put off. Tasks we do finish because we drove ourselves too hard burn us out, leaving us without energy for whatever else needs to be done.

This exercise forces you to focus on the process of doing the task, not on the outcome of getting the task done. In the doing, you can find your flow, allowing curiosity and inspiration to reveal themselves. When we're not driving ourselves to finish, we can work in a relaxed state and rest when necessary. Your expansive mind-set will be: *It is okay to start things without finishing them. My survival is not at stake!*

When the timer goes off, and you haven't completed a task, you will feel irritation. *Just two more minutes and I could cross this off my list!* You may also feel anxiety about what will happen with the task incomplete. *If I don't answer these emails, people will think I'm ignoring them!* Your limbic system is signaling that you're under threat, just as you expected. Welcome these false alarms. Whatever happens, you can handle it. This is how you break the perfectionist cycle of anxiety.

★ We're accustomed to feeling relief when a task is done, and you're going to miss that today. Take extra care to reward yourself for what you *are* doing: stopping when the timer goes off, thinking expansively, and making space for negative emotion. Move your self-compassion band, give yourself a loving pat, and tell yourself, *Good job!*

Taylor, the lifeguard at our local municipal pool, gets up at 4:30 a.m. so she can unlock the gate and prepare the facility before swimmers arrive. One chilly December morning, while rolling up the massive pool covers, she slipped and fell in the water. Sopping wet and shivering, she stayed for our lap swim without complaint.

The next time I went swimming, to show my gratitude, I brought a dozen holiday cookies to the pool for Taylor. It's hard to imagine anything to criticize with this act of kindness, but my perfectionistic monkey mind had no trouble. Here's what popped out of my mouth when I gave them to Taylor:

"I'm not much of a baker. They might be overcooked."

"I don't know if you'll like them. They're vegan."

"It's been a couple of days since I made them, so they might be stale."

Taylor, of course, was having none of it. She shook her head at my excuses and thanked me with a huge smile. And to my surprise, a week later she asked me for the recipe!

Is it hard to please your inner critic? In tomorrow's exercise you'll learn what to do when you can't get no satisfaction.

Cope with Criticism 3

Today you'll engage in an imaginal conversation with your biggest critic—the voice in your head. Since we perfectionists are our own worst critics, we can easily play both roles in the exchange. The subject of this debate could be something you've done in the past that provoked real or imagined criticism. Or it could be something you're afraid to do for fear of being criticized. While you could do this exercise entirely in your head, you'll get a better workout if you write the conversation down. Download the Cope with Criticism workout sheet first, then follow these steps.

1. Write down what you did, or might do, that will be the object for criticism.

2. Imagine the worst thing anyone could think or say about you. You could play your own critic, or you could identify a person in your life who might be likely to criticize you. (For example, if I didn't know a diagnosis for a certain mental health disorder and asked a colleague what it was, I might imagine them saying or thinking, *If you don't know this diagnosis, you couldn't be much of a clinician!*)

3. Think up an assertive response to the criticism. You don't need to convince the critic they're wrong, or get defensive or aggressive. Just stand up for yourself. This

works best if you first acknowledge what is true about the judgment. (Using my example, I could say: "While it's true I don't know this particular diagnosis, good clinicians seek out answers to what they don't know.")

4. Now imagine what your critic might say or think in response to your assertive statement, and stand up for yourself again. Repeat this back-and-forth exchange until you can't think of any more criticism.

Because we cannot garner others' approval all the time, criticism is an inevitable part of life. Yet, as perfectionists, we treat criticism as evidence that we have failed in some way, and we'll do anything to prevent it. This happens even when the criticism is only imagined. This thinking is a sure sign that we've been hijacked. The monkey mind is so concerned with the potential judgments—and possible rejection—of others that it acts as a mind reader, conjuring up any possible criticism and using it to edit our behavior. The monkey mind-set is, *I am only secure as long as there is nothing to criticize about me.*

To move forward with your goals and values, you need to be able to cope with occasional criticism. Self-assertion skills will help. With practice, you'll become more resilient in the face of others' negative judgments—real and perceived—and more self-compassionate when the criticism is accurate. You can even learn to welcome criticism so you can learn from your mistakes. And eventually you will develop coping skills to such an extent that you'll feel confident enough to take bigger and bigger risks despite what others might think or say. The expansive mind-set you want to cultivate is, *Criticism is not a sign I have done something wrong. When I am acting in accordance with my values, I can handle it.* Over time this will become your default way of thinking.

Most of the negative judgments we imagine others are making about us are projections of the negative judgments we make of ourselves. Knowing this doesn't make them any easier to discount. That's because any criticism, real or imagined, can bring up anger, guilt, and shame. Feeling these emotions during this exercise is to be expected; they are neurochemical cocktails served up by your limbic system, beyond your control. Your best response is to welcome them and allow them to work their way through your system. When you do this, you're training the monkey to understand that you can handle criticism and the emotions that come along with it.

The goal in this exercise is to bring awareness to the self-criticism you habitually engage in, and to address it with mindful dialogue. Each time you imagine your critic's voice, move your self-compassion band. Each time you stand up for yourself in response, move it again. Praise yourself for the higher values you're aiming for, like honesty, openness, authenticity, and courage. And give yourself extra points for using the workout sheet!

Do you tend to reread your texts, emails, and social media posts to make sure there are no typos or other mistakes? Do you get anxious when you press send, fearing you missed something that will make you look like a fool? Tomorrow you'll practice making a mistake as a way to embrace yourself. It's the only way to develop true confidence!

Make a Messaging Mistake

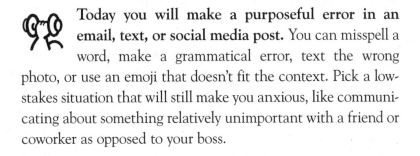

Today you will make a purposeful error in an email, text, or social media post. You can misspell a word, make a grammatical error, text the wrong photo, or use an emoji that doesn't fit the context. Pick a low-stakes situation that will still make you anxious, like communicating about something relatively unimportant with a friend or coworker as opposed to your boss.

The monkey mind is great at reacting quickly to imminent threats to our survival, but when it comes to the risks involved in online communications, it tends to overestimate the possibility that we'll be judged harshly and lose social status due to misspellings and other mistakes. It also underestimates our ability to recover if we do draw criticism. Hijacked by our limbic system, the perfectionist's unconscious mind-set is, *Making a mistake means I'm less worthy.*

If we want to learn to engage spontaneously or authentically with others, we must adopt an expansive mind-set: *Social communication mistakes are inevitable, and if I'm judged harshly for making one, I can handle it.* With repeated practice of this exercise, you'll have a better perspective on the actual consequences of hitting the wrong key or forgetting to add an attachment. This perspective will help you be more relaxed when communicating with others and will decrease rumination over past errors. By allowing mistakes you will become more open, vulnerable, spontaneous, and authentic, all qualities that foster true connection with others.

Regardless of whether your intentional social mistake draws criticism, you're likely to experience anxiety, embarrassment, and even shame over how the other person reacts. By welcoming these emotions with your breath, rather than resisting them, you can train the limbic system to be less reactive in the future. Every time you think about your mistake and feel discomfort, move your self-compassion band, take a deep breath, and remind yourself of your expansive mind-set. When we allow enough space for these feelings, they tend to evaporate.

The most important aspect of this practice is to learn to forgive yourself for making mistakes. If, in fact, someone points out your error or teases you, don't defend yourself or make the excuse that you did it purposely. Instead, use your new expansive mind-set to compose a reply, such as, "Yes, I did make a mistake. Guess I'm human after all!" Add a heart emoji, hit send, and move your self-compassion band again.

In the eleventh grade, I wrote a research paper about Maria Montessori, a pioneer in early childhood education. I loved reading biographies about her and her own writing on her education philosophy. I loved filling out dozens and dozens of index cards with all the details I would put in my paper. But writing the paper itself was a different matter. I wasn't confident in my ability to express my ideas in a clear, concise way, let alone use correct grammar and spelling. Every time I began to write I tensed up. I wrote a sentence, then crossed it out. I wrote another, then crossed that out, finally settling on something that still did not seem quite right. I finished the paper the night before it was due, thoroughly disappointed with myself. I was so embarrassed to hand it in the next morning that I hurriedly wrote a note of apology to my teacher, telling him how unhappy I was with the paper, and how much I wished I could have done the subject justice.

Several days later our papers were returned, marked and graded, but mine had some additional comments. "I gave your apology note an A+. I suspect that were you not so concerned with your writing ability, I would have given you the same on your paper. In the future, I suggest you stop apologizing and trust your own voice."

His words of encouragement have stuck with me. Now, whenever I sit down to write and my old insecurities arrive to greet me, I expect them. Feeling fear and doubt are part of my writing workout, and sweating them away is one of the most satisfying things I do in my life. After a writing session, I feel a kind of mental endorphin high for the rest *of the day. My writing sessions make me a better clinician, more creative and clear minded in my work.*

Do you have an internal critic who believes your writing is never good enough? Do you put off writing until you feel confident and clear minded, which often means putting it off indefinitely? If so, tomorrow's practice is for you!

Today you are going to write for fifteen minutes without stopping, editing, or judging what you've written. You'll set a timer, then begin moving your pen on the paper or your fingers on the keyboard, and continue until the timer goes off. The subject you write about doesn't matter; however, it might help to choose something you're interested in, such as a hobby, personal project, or relationship. If nothing comes to mind, try writing about a dream you had, a memory, something you're happy or sad about, or the process of writing itself. If you get stuck, write, "I don't know what to write, I don't know what to write," until something pops into your mind, and then go with that.

Peter Elbow developed this concept of *freewriting* in 1973, and it remains one of the most powerful exercises for undermining perfectionism. Freed from the burden of correct grammar and spelling, and from sounding clever or smart, people are often surprised by how prolific they can be when they write without the constraint of doing it "right."

For most of us, our first experience with writing was in school, where our handwriting, spelling, grammar, and organization of ideas were graded. With our innate desire to secure the attention and respect of teachers and parents, being graded raised the stakes, triggering the limbic system's fight-or-flight alarms telling us we better get it right. We learned to think, *If what I write isn't good, it means I am not good.* This monkey mind-set devalues our higher values in favor of playing it safe. Instead of feeling motivated by the joy of self-expression, we're motivated by the fear of being judged as a failure. Is it any wonder we feel insecure when we sit down to write?

Writing "freely" in this exercise does not mean writing well. In fact, when I coach clients using freewriting, I often encourage them to write poorly. We want to activate our monkey mind-set so we can counter it with an expansive mind-set: *I can act and express myself with unconditional self-acceptance.*

This way of thinking will allow us to express ourselves spontaneously, to take risks, and perhaps to even find creative flow. Should we write something that provokes criticism, that's okay; our expansive mind-set allows for mistakes. Making mistakes is how we humans learn and grow to reach our full potential.

Of course, when you provoke the monkey, you're going to get a neurological call to action. Freewriting brings up performance anxiety; you feel you must stop and make sure you're writing coherently and correctly. You may feel foggy and confused, unsure of what to write at all. You'll likely feel as if there is too much at stake to risk writing another word. Welcome all these feelings with open arms. They are part of the writing process, and you must allow them to work themselves out on their own. And while they do, you can practice self-compassion.

⭐ Remember, don't get sucked into evaluating the quality or quantity of your output. The purpose is to tame your monkey mind. Give yourself praise when you feel the anxiety, and continue writing anyway. While it is true that freewriting will make you a better writer, that's not what you're after today.

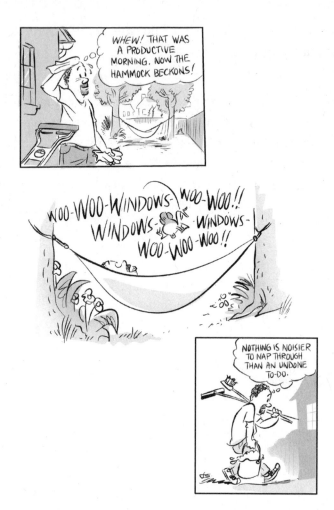

Do you feel overwhelmed and stressed by all that you need to get done? Do you get down on yourself for the tasks you didn't get to, and discount what you did accomplish? And do you habitually overestimate what you think you can get done in the time you have? If you'd like to ease up on yourself, decrease your stress, and feel more worthwhile and deserving, then tomorrow's exercise is for you!

List Your To-Don'ts

6

In addition to making a normal to-do list today, you'll make a list of tasks you're *not* going to do. To qualify for this to-don't list, a task must be one that you want to get done and would otherwise be on your list of things to do. Today, what you *don't* do will be more important than what you do. Here are examples of my lists:

> To-do list: spend one hour writing this exercise, do laundry, spend one hour preparing for a presentation on Monday, go to the gym, and go out to dinner with some friends.

> To-don't list: house cleaning, grocery shopping, prepping for my week's lunches, and going to the post office to mail a package.

To some, it might seem like I'll have an easier time of it this way, but if you knew me, you'd know how hard *not* doing these tasks will be for me.

As perfectionists, our sense of self-worth is closely tied to how much we get done. If we don't complete every task that lies ahead, we must not have worked hard enough. If we don't meet all our obligations, we'll be judged and criticized. To the monkey mind, not working hard enough and failing to meet obligations could lead to others' judgments, even rejection, and so it sounds the alarm. When we react by pushing ourselves harder, or by mentally punishing ourselves for falling short, we're feeding the monkey, reinforcing the monkey mind-set of *I am only worthy if I get it all done*. This conditional self-acceptance keeps us overwhelmed and in a perpetual cycle of stress.

Today's exercise will teach you three important things. First, that you deserve praise for the tasks you get done, even when there are more left to do. Second, that you can set clear and reasonable limits on what you expect of yourself (and you'll praise yourself for that too). Third, that positive reinforcement works better than negative reinforcement (and as such, you'll praise the doing and the not doing equally). By placing realistic expectations on yourself and practicing self-care, you're reinforcing a more expansive mind-set: *I am worthy even if I don't get it all done*.

With this mind-set, you'll create a better balance between work, rest, and play, resulting in fewer overwhelming feelings and less self-judgment. You'll create the possibility for more energy and joy in your life. By using positive reinforcement, you'll cultivate self-compassion and unconditional self-acceptance, the essential ingredients for feelings of positive self-worth.

Today's exercise intentionally robs you of the feeling of accomplishment you have when you get one more thing done. This will likely provoke feelings of irritation, anxiety, and inadequacy. These emotions are noise, not a signal that you're under threat. By expecting and accepting these feelings, you're sending the message to your monkey mind that you are safe, even with to-dos remaining. As you exercise your welcoming breath, the monkey mind will calm down, and you'll learn to trust that you don't need to do it all to feel good about yourself.

☆ If we criticized our children for what they didn't get done, without praising what they did get done, we'd be programming them to feel insecure and inadequate. Be a good parent to yourself today. You'll be breaking an old habit and creating a new one, so you'll need lots of encouragement. Be very generous in praising yourself for what you do and don't do today. Every time you feel the urge to do one more thing, move your self-compassion band. If you chose not to make the bed today, every time you see it or think of it, pat yourself on the back for a job not done!

For the first two decades of my private practice, instead of ending sessions after the standard fifty minutes, I allowed them to keep going, sometimes right up until the last minute. No sooner was one client out the door than another was coming in. I scrambled to switch from one set of notes to the next, and bathroom breaks were like fire drills. But I felt that I owed it to my clients. Sending them away so I could relax seemed like such a self-indulgent thing to do. I felt that I'd be shortchanging my clients if I denied them precious minutes that held the potential for additional insight and healing.

But I was shortchanging myself. The cumulative stress of working back-to-back sessions without a real break wore on me. I wasn't enjoying my work as much and felt like booking fewer clients. I had a case of burnout, one of the biggest red flags for perfectionism. Here I was, treating clients for perfectionism, simultaneously modeling perfectionist behavior myself!

Gradually I reclaimed those ten minutes every hour to organize and reenergize myself. I put aside five minutes to finish and file notes and prepare for the next session. But even more important were the five minutes of sacred space I devoted to physical movement, like jumping jacks, stretching, resistance band exercises, or even taking a brief walk outside. Taking a more active break to completely disengage from work improved my energy and focus, not only during sessions but also at home. And since I see five clients on a typical workday, my new take-a-break strategy added a total of twenty-five minutes of exercise to my day. What a bonus!

Do you tend to plow your way through your tasks and projects, only stopping when you burn out? Tomorrow's exercise will increase motivation, creativity, mental clarity, and the ability to make decisions, and it will improve your health, in just five minutes!

7 Reboot! Reboot! Reboot!

 **Today you will take a five-minute break after every twenty-five minutes of work.** Whether you're working at a computer, cleaning house, or shoveling snow, you'll stop every twenty-five minutes regardless of whether the task is done. During each break, you can do nearly anything you choose other than the work itself. I suggest something physical, like stretching, walking, or going up and down an empty stairwell; however, you may prefer to make a cup of tea or meditate. What's important is to stop working and reboot.

While you can use your phone's built-in timer, I suggest downloading one of the many free apps available to help you track each work session. I rely on one when I'm writing, and as it happens, it just signaled that it's time for a break. Think I'll put on some music and dance!

To our limbic system, our survival is tied to working long and hard. For our ancestors it meant hunting and gathering and keeping an eye out for predators. As a result, our monkey mind has a built-in bias against work breaks; we consciously associate them with laziness. The perfectionist's monkey mind-set is, *Breaks are a nonessential indulgence and will interfere with productivity.*

Sitting or standing in place for hours at a time takes a serious toll on our physical and mental health. Our increasingly sedentary workforce is subject to more heart disease, diabetes, depression, and obesity than previous, more active generations. And recent research correlates working without breaks with poorer decision-making ability and decreased concentration. Sacrificing our health—physical *and* mental—doesn't make us more productive.

Breaks are a productivity enhancer. Simply standing up from our desk and walking around improves circulation, tones our muscles, and boosts our metabolism. We can return to the job with improved focus, decision-making clarity, and renewed motivation. The expansive mind-set we want to grow is, *I can be more creative and productive, as well as healthier, when I take frequent breaks.*

Our limbic system has conditioned us to plow through tasks without stopping, and it won't agree to take a rest when we decide to. It will take real discipline to stop what you're doing when your timer goes off. You will feel frustrated at having to leave something undone while it seems like the rest of the world is leaving you in the dust. You'll wonder whether these breaks will mean you won't finish what needs to get finished today. The timer may sound irritating to you, like it's bossing you around. All these feelings are to be expected and welcomed. Breathing deeply and slowly, place your hand on your heart and know that you deserve to reboot.

⭐ Old work habits are hard to change, even for a few hours. If you don't successfully take sixteen breaks in your eight-hour workday, that's okay. You may need to dial it down to an hour between breaks, or even longer. Give yourself lots of encouragement every time you succeed in a reboot. Use your self-compassion band to remind yourself what you're after with this practice: better health, increased focus, more creativity.

Are there things that you intend to do but keep putting off? Do you think the reason you procrastinate is because you're lazy? Nothing could be further from the truth, which is that you're so invested in doing tasks well that the pressure of perfection becomes aversive. Don't worry—tomorrow's exercise will help you deal with that.

8 Jumpstart It!

Today you will spend five minutes beginning a task you have been putting off. The task might be a tedious chore, like tackling that pile of unanswered emails, a stack of bills, or a quarterly report. It could be a personal project, like organizing your workspace or cleaning the gutters. Or it might be a lifestyle change, like taking up an exercise or meditation practice. Rather than postpone the task or worry about it anymore, you'll set a timer for five minutes and, without thinking too much, *jumpstart it!*

When the timer goes off, stop. That's it. It doesn't matter how much of the task you got done or how imperfectly it was done. If you feel motivated to continue, you may do so, but otherwise move on with the rest of your day. Either way, you get 100 percent credit for jumpstarting the task.

Chances are you've thought of yourself as too busy or too lazy to get around to this task, but the more likely culprit is your perfectionism. To the monkey mind, doing anything less than perfectly leaves us vulnerable to criticism, from ourselves and possibly others. Physical exercise must be done with grace and stamina, or we should stay on the couch. Meditation should be done without fidgeting and for at least thirty minutes, or we're posers. Emails must have good grammar, intelligence, and humor, or we're stupid. And since leaving any task unfinished could draw criticism, we should never start what we can't finish. The monkey mind-set is, *If I cannot do it perfectly, I shouldn't do it at all.*

The expansive mind-set you'll adopt for this exercise is, *Five minutes of* doing *is better than five minutes of avoiding.* Inspiration is more likely to strike you when you're in action rather than idle. And by taking action, even when you don't feel like it, you send a clear message to the monkey: *no banana!* Today you are feeding your own values of flexibility, creativity, commitment, patience, and courage.

There is a wide range of emotions that may arise when we begin a task we aren't inspired to do. If it has a learning curve, or will be difficult, you may feel anxiety, even dread. It the task doesn't physically or mentally engage you, boredom will immediately set in. If it's a big task that will take a long time to complete, you may feel overwhelmed. You might even resent having to do the task in the first place, or feel foolish setting a timer for yourself. And of course, you may ask yourself, *If I only spend five minutes on it now, when will I finish it?* which could provoke more anxiety. These feelings are all a natural function of our limbic system. Rather than resist them by avoiding the task any longer, you're going to welcome them with your breath and embrace the task for a few minutes.

☆ It will be tempting to grade yourself for how much you got done in five minutes or how well you did it, but the purpose of this exercise is just to jumpstart yourself. There will be no second-guessing or quality control today. Reward yourself for the emotions you welcomed and for the expansive mind-set you cultivated. And if you should begin to feel inspired to engage more deeply with the task, give yourself a bonus point!

A couple of years ago one of my sons landed a job as a research engineer at a start-up in Seattle. It was his dream job in his dream town, but when he checked in with me at the end of the first week he sounded uncharacteristically unsure of himself. Everyone was so smart and everything was so new, he told me; at meetings, he couldn't follow everything. If he asked questions, he thought he would sound stupid. He wondered whether he was qualified for his position.

It was a clear case of imposter syndrome. We cannot learn enough to be comfortable in new situations without asking questions. To be comfortable at his job, my son would have to get comfortable feeling stupid. So, we made an agreement. Every time he went to the grocery store, he had to ask an employee a question. By the end of the first month he knew the difference between cilantro and parsley, a sweet onion and a yellow onion, romaine lettuce and green lettuce. I was not only pleased that he was facing his fear but that he was shopping for produce!

The experience taught him it was okay to ask questions, even ones that might've seemed stupid. Before long my son was asking work colleagues questions about projects he was working on. He was surprised to discover how often his were questions that nobody had answers for and that needed to be openly expressed and addressed. Having the courage to look stupid turned out to be the smart thing to do. It made him a more valuable part of his team.

Do you hesitate to let others know that you don't know? Rather than ask a question that might appear "stupid," do you just play along until you can find the answer on your own? The next exercise will help you build the confidence you need to admit you don't know everything.

Ask a Stupid Question

Today you will ask somebody a question that you already know, or think you *should* know, the answer to. Ask the grocer if they have low-fat milk. Stand across the street from a coffee shop and ask someone where the nearest coffee shop is. Ask a coworker how to pronounce "Alzheimer's," or, "What's the difference between snow and hail?" Depending on what you ask and who you ask, you will get different levels of anxiety with this exercise, so choose a situation you think you can tolerate. If you don't get enough of a workout, you can always follow up with a question that's even "stupider"!

Intelligence is often associated with knowledge—the more we know, the more intelligent we are, right? But they are not the same. *Knowledge* is the accumulation of information. *Intelligence* is how well we use that information. The limbic system can't make this distinction, and when we encounter an unknown, the monkey mind-set is activated: *If I don't know something, I am stupid.* We think we must appear knowledgeable or we'll lose the respect of others. When we're afraid to reveal what we don't know, it becomes very difficult to acquire new information. This is not an intelligent way to think and act!

Being candid about what we don't know honors our higher values of being more open, vulnerable, and curious, values that encourage our own learning, and creates more opportunities for connection with others. In general, people like to share knowledge with each other; it makes us feel useful and fosters community. The expansive mind-set you want to feed with this exercise is, *Asking questions is not only smart, but it helps me connect authentically with others.*

Since there is always the possibility that someone might say something mean or laugh at us when we ask a question, shame and embarrassment are bound to come up. This exercise will purposely activate these emotions, and you need to take a welcoming stance toward them. If you begin to shake, sweat, or blush when you ask a question, open your hands, open your chest and heart, and breathe into this discomfort. If someone reacts in a way that makes you feel a little silly or embarrassed, breathe into those sensations too. This is how we build the resilience and self-compassion we need to thrive despite our less-than-perfect knowledge of the world around us.

If nobody smirks or rolls their eyes at your question today, naturally you'll feel relieved. But remember to reward yourself for taking the risk, regardless of the outcome. If at any point in the day you get a jolt of shame thinking about the question you asked, remind yourself of how brave you are, lavish praise on yourself, and move your self-compassion band. And if you had a particularly painful exchange with someone, you can revisit the Cope with Criticism exercise from earlier in this book for extra credit!

Would you like to be more relaxed and experience more joy and fun in your life? For the perfectionist this will take practice, something tomorrow's exercise will offer.

Whether it's a weekend or a workday, today your assignment is to schedule some time for fun. You might go for a hike, take a drive, go out to eat, or visit a museum. You could make time for a neglected hobby like gardening, gaming, crafting, or bird-watching. Any leisure activity will do—reading, playing games, listening to music, or hanging out with family or friends. No matter how busy your day looks, block off at least fifteen minutes for some play.

From the perspective of the monkey mind, playing and having fun are dangerous detours from the straight-and-narrow path of survival. If we give in to fun, it will distract us from getting things done and making a living. All we'll want to do is play and be irresponsible, fun-loving losers. The monkey mind-set is, *Unless all my work is done, there is no time for play.*

The problem with this thinking is that by the time our work is done, we don't have the energy for play. Play is clinically proven to be essential for brain development, managing stress, trauma recovery, and developing healthy relationships, not only in children but in adults as well. The expansive mind-set we want today is, *Playtime is essential to stay mentally and physically healthy.*

Simple as it may sound, scheduling a little fun into your day can be a challenge when you're not used to doing so. You may feel irritated at having to interrupt your important tasks. You might feel that play is self-indulgent and childish—*I'm too old for this!*—and worry about the work you're not getting done. Don't be hijacked by these negative emotions; think of them as growing pains as you learn to reclaim your natural ability to play. Breathe into these feelings and remind yourself of your expansive mind-set. You not only have the right to a little fun, you have an obligation to yourself to keep your life in balance.

If you don't have any fun while playing today, remember that it was an *exercise*, meaning it is difficult and will take practice to master. Be gentle on yourself. Move your self-compassion band and give yourself a pat on the back for making time for play!

Many of my clients suffer from a type of perfectionism called social anxiety, *which is the fear of being judged, criticized, and rejected because of how we look and act. They manage this anxiety by withdrawing from social interactions. One young man, a stocky ex-football player, had become so self-conscious in public places that he was about to drop out of college. After a session or two in my office, he agreed to an exercise far more challenging than three laps around the football field: three laps around the mall wearing a lovely pink flower-dappled woman's scarf. As I wrapped it around his neck, I reminded him to be sure to hit the food court.*

"This is crazy. I don't think I can do this," he said. But after a little coaching and coaxing, off he went.

Ten minutes later he returned, visibly shaking and sweating. "I'm pretty sure everyone's giving me weird looks," he said.

"That's great," I said. "Just what we want. Remember, your goal is to accept yourself, even if others don't."

When he returned from his second lap, he looked more relaxed. "It wasn't so bad this time," he said. "I'm not even sure most people noticed."

His third lap took twenty minutes. When I asked what took him so long, he told me he stopped off at the shoe store to try on some cross-trainers—still wearing the bright, flowery woman's scarf! "The clerk gave me a funny look, but so what?" he said. "That's his problem, not mine!"

I gave him a high five for his courage. It was probably just as tough a workout as he'd ever had on a football field.

Would you like to develop unconditional acceptance of yourself? Would you like to free yourself from your inner critic? Would you like to judge less and love more? Tomorrow's practice will help you do this.

Wear Something Weird

Wear something you will be embarrassed to be seen in today! Remember pajama day or weird hair day in elementary school? It was fun and different, and relatively safe, because everyone was doing it. Today it will just be you!

You could wear striped slacks with a polka-dotted blouse, a tacky T-shirt, an out-of-style coat, even a piece of clothing inside out. If you can't find something in your closet, borrow from your spouse or roommate. It doesn't matter what you choose as long as it makes you uncomfortably self-conscious.

What we wear and how we present ourselves is important. Every culture has its own set of customs about what is appropriate to wear. For example, at a funeral in the United States, people generally wear black, and if you showed up in a bright-pink outfit you'd be considered rude or insensitive. Today's practice is not meant to violate these types of customs. Rather, the intent is to be purposely imperfect, activating the overly sensitive monkey mind that believes, *If I don't look perfect and people criticize me for this, I'm less worthy.* The belief that mistakes make us less worthy than others causes excessive stress and anxiety. And this may manifest as spending too much money and time on clothing, or it may get in the way of taking risks and dressing authentically.

Today you're going to break the rules you've imposed on yourself and exercise your higher values. Rather than letting the monkey's values dictate your dress, you'll be spontaneous and grab a random hat or scarf. You'll be creative and wear your husband's shirt, or you'll be authentic and wear a heavy sweater, even if it's summer. The expansive mind-set you'll be cultivating is, *How I dress doesn't determine my worth as a person. If people judge me, I can cope.*

Even if choosing clothes is not an area of stress for you, this exercise will likely make you uncomfortable. Transgressing any cultural norm fires up the limbic system, so expect to experience anxiety, embarrassment, even shame. Don't try to resist feeling these emotions or avoid them by changing back to something safer. Instead, expand around them with your breath and give them all the space they want. This tells the monkey mind, *I can handle this.* Developing resilience to what we feel internally is how we build resilience to external criticism, freeing us to dress to please ourselves.

You may get some looks or comments from others today; if so, great! The more critical, the better the workout you're getting. Regardless of how others react, give yourself plenty of praise for the risk you're taking, for the emotions you're welcoming, and for the higher values you're expressing. Move your self-compassion band and tell yourself that you are so courageous! This is self-compassion in action.

Do compliments make you feel uncomfortable? Do you tend to qualify whatever it is the person complimented? Tomorrow's exercise will not only help you to feel better about yourself, it will also make the person who complimented you feel good.

THE ONLY THING HARDER
THAN MAKING EXCUSES
ON A BAD HAIR DAY IS
FIELDING COMPLIMENTS
ON A GOOD HAIR DAY.

Accept a Compliment **12**

Whenever you receive a compliment today, respond with a simple thank you. Whether it's a positive comment about your appearance or a task you performed, or praise for your child, mate, or pet, receive it with grace. Don't qualify the compliment! For example, if someone compliments you on your child's good behavior at the supermarket, don't chuckle and say, "You should see him *before* his nap. It's a different story!" If a coworker congratulates you for nailing that presentation, don't roll the credits announcing all the help you got. Whenever you hear praise today, even if it's dead wrong and you're certain you don't deserve it, just smile and say, "Thank you, that is lovely to hear!"

Compliments are a lot better than criticism, so why is accepting them an issue? While we want to be praised, being praised can make us the center of attention, exposing us to heightened scrutiny. *Woo-woo-woo!* When others see us in the spotlight, what will they see and think about our lesser qualities? And what if the compliment is too generous, going beyond our own sense of accomplishment and confidence? It's a reminder of our own inadequacies, and it points to new, higher expectations of us in the future. *Woo-woo-woo!* And what if the person who is complimenting actually feels pity for us and is trying to give us a friendly boost? *Woo-woo-woo!* And if I say thanks, won't I seem stuck-up? *Woo-woo-woo!*

The only way to eliminate these "threats" to our personal security is to deserve every compliment that we receive. In other words, be perfect. Our monkey mind-set is, *Unless I am consistently perfect, it's not safe to be admired or appreciated.* Stuck in our hopeless quest for perfection, we can never pause and feel good about what we've done, or build a healthy sense of self-esteem. Every time we qualify a compliment, we not only feed the monkey, we rob the person who complimented us of the satisfaction of praising us.

When we accept a compliment, we feed ourselves, not the monkey. Our expansive mind-set is, *I deserve to be admired and appreciated. I am good enough as I am in this moment.* Compliments are an important way to remind each other of this essential truth. When we accept a compliment with grace, we're not only building self-acceptance and fostering positive feelings about ourselves; we're also appreciating the one who gave the compliment, helping them feel positive about themselves. This is a powerful way to build connection and belonging, the very things we need to survive.

You may be surprised how hard it is to resist the urge to qualify a compliment. If it happens in a group, you may feel embarrassed being singled out. If you receive praise for looking, behaving, or producing better than you have in the past, you may feel enhanced pressure and fear that others will expect the same from you from now on. Or you may mistrust the motives of the person giving the compliment, and experience doubt or resentment. Compliments can even feel patronizing and bring up feelings of shame. Your workout is to welcome these feelings with your breath and body unconditionally. They are the false alarms of the hungry monkey, howling to be fed.

☆ For many of us, qualifying compliments is a reflex. If this describes you, go easy on yourself. It is a hard habit to break. You can always recover by saying, "Thank you, that is nice to hear." Move your self-compassion band for recognizing your reflex, again for your recovery, and once more for reminding yourself of your expansive mind-set. You can rewire your old perfectionistic habits, one compliment at a time.

For most of my life I started my day by making a list of all the chores, tasks, and obligations I believed I needed to get done that day. My list was like a compass, always pointing me in the right direction. Then, a few years ago at the end of a particularly productive day, instead of celebrating all I'd accomplished, I found myself complaining to my husband that I hadn't had time that day to take a lunch break, go to the gym, or meet with a friend.

That night I decided, Tomorrow, I'll go without a list. I knew it would be good practice for me, because the very thought of "going list-less" made me incredibly anxious. Although it was a Saturday with no work-related obligations, I felt so lost that morning that I made a list anyway! But not wanting to fail completely, I threw it away. All that day I was like a pilot flying blind. I was so used to getting things done according to an agenda that I had little sense of what I wanted to do. Painful as that day was, being untethered gave me a hint of freedom. I decided to try losing the list again the next day.

I went a whole year without making a list. I got more in touch with what I wanted to do, rather than focusing on what I should do. And, over time, when I forgot to get something done, it became easier for me to forgive myself. I'd learned how to recognize my heart's desire, which is a better compass than any list.

Are you lost without a list? Can you relax only after you have everything checked off? To practice feeling more free and spontaneous, and to have more fun, go to the next exercise!

Lose the List 13

Go a day without making a list. Whether you normally make a list of the whole day's events, or just a shopping list, go without it today. There will be a void where you are accustomed to structure; see if you can tune in to your internal inspiration for what to do next. This is a good exercise to do on a weekend or a day off, when the cost of forgetting a task doesn't have consequences that negatively affect clients or coworkers.

There is nothing inherently wrong with making lists, but for perfectionists, regular list-making can support a hidden belief system that robs us of our ability to relax and be present. If you refrain from making a list before you embark on your day or your shopping trip, unconscious assumptions may come to light: *Without a list my life will fall apart, I'll lose control, I won't get anything done, I'll forget things and let people down.* The monkey mind-set is, *If I'm not organized, I cannot relax.* This task-oriented mentality doesn't acknowledge inspiration, spontaneity, creativity, or our need for self-care. And when we think this way, obstacles tend to irritate us. We see others as instruments to help us get things done, and we get impatient when they fail to meet our expectations. When opportunities to rest, play, or socialize come along, we're too busy to take advantage of them.

Without a list to follow, we are more likely to stop jumping compulsively to the next to-do, and space opens up for new experiences. If an obstacle to getting a task done should arise, we can choose to be flexible and creative, perhaps circling around to the task later. When others don't cooperate, we can be patient and present with them. We're more likely to notice opportunities to be spontaneous, doing things that feed ourselves rather than the monkey. The expansive mind-set we want to create is, *When I let go of control, I can be in flow.*

Without your go-to guide telling you what to do next, you may feel confused, helpless, and alone. Like an explorer in uncharted territory, you'll need courage to stay the course. This doesn't mean you need to grit your teeth and plow ahead—just the opposite. Expand your internal space to make room for the feelings that arise, such as fear that you're not getting enough done, that you're forgetting what's important, and that something bad will happen. If you forget something—and you will—you may feel regret or self-doubt; you may even shame yourself for being "lazy." Whatever the emotion, breathe deliberately and deeply, welcoming it with self-compassion. It can't last forever, and you've got all day!

The monkey mind will try to trick you into following a *mental* list to compensate for your missing written list. Remember, this exercise is not about getting everything done without a written list; it's about discovering the inner desires that we miss when we follow an external agenda. You earn stars today for (1) embracing your expansive mind-set, and (2) for allowing emotions to metabolize on their own without resisting them. There are *no stars* for maintaining your usual level of productivity.

Without a list, odds are you won't get everything done. When I started this practice five years ago, I would get down on myself for forgetting something important. I had to remind myself again and again that productivity loss is part of the exercise. So, when you forget something, move your self-compassion band, give yourself a bonus star, and congratulate yourself for your day of list-less-ness.

Do you have trouble making up your mind because you're worried you'll choose the wrong thing? Would you like to become more relaxed, decisive, and flexible? Tomorrow's playful practice will help you do this.

Flip a Coin **14**

For any situation today that offers two options, flip a coin. Eat in or eat out? Red shoes or blue? Check email or read a book? Make them all heads or tails decisions today. Keep this practice low stakes. Don't try to plan your next vacation destination with a coin!

Having to choose between two things is stressful when we think there is a "right" choice. What if we choose "wrong"? *If I eat out, I'll spend too much money. If I wear red shoes, I won't look good in them. If I read a book, I'll fall behind in my email.* To make matters worse, our hyperactive limbic system will second-guess whatever choice we make. For example, if you eat in, you may not enjoy the food; if you wear the blue shoes, your outfit may be too boring; if you read email, you'll never get around to the book you want to read. There is no pleasing the monkey mind!

When we're hijacked, our mind-set is, *I can't afford to make a mistake.* We not only have trouble making decisions, but because every choice has a downside, we tend to get down on ourselves whatever decision we make.

By flipping a coin to choose between two options, we expand our mind-set to allow for either outcome. We're saying, *Whatever decision I make is okay. I can cope with the outcome*. Freed from responsibility to make the right choice, we can move ahead quickly, without procrastinating, and focus on what's important: embracing our decision and coping with the consequences. Coin flipping will probably lead to choices you wouldn't normally make, but you'll be acting more spontaneously, taking more risks, and acting more creatively. With enough of this exercise, you'll come to see that what you choose is much less important than how you respond to what the choice entails.

Although this is a low-stakes practice, don't be surprised if it brings up unpleasant emotions. You may feel annoyance with the randomness of coin flipping, anxiety about whether you made a mistake, or grief over the loss of what you didn't choose. These emotions are not a sign that you made a bad choice; they're a sign that this exercise is good for you, and one to be repeated. Take a deep breath. Welcome whatever you feel, and remind yourself that the only mistake is thinking there is a perfect choice.

Often, after making a choice by the flip of a coin, it will become very clear to you that you wanted the other option. Curb your urge to go back on your decision. Learning how to cope with the outcome of your choice is what you're after today. If things turn out poorly, congratulations! You'll have even more opportunity to practice self-compassion and acceptance. Move your self-compassion band or give yourself a pat on the back.

Michaela came into therapy with the goal of reducing the stress in her life. With a full-time profession and her husband, Larry, and two young children to care for, she was overwhelmed, often getting as little as five hours of sleep a night. It quickly became clear to me that Michaela was doing more than her fair share of work around the house, and it wasn't because Larry wasn't willing and able to do more. She wouldn't allow him to do more.

Whenever Larry took initiative with the children by getting them ready for school, helping them with their homework, or taking them to the park, Michaela subtly undermined him and took over. It was the same with housework; Larry didn't cook or clean well enough to suit her. Michaela was a self-described "control freak."

To help Michaela learn how to let go of control, we identified little tasks that were contributing to her stress that she'd be willing to delegate. After several weeks of practice with letting go of tasks like making sandwiches, vacuuming the living room, and putting the kids to bed, Michaela was making progress. Then one week she described a big stressor: her eight-year-old son's birthday party was approaching, and she was busy preparing for a work conference. After much anguish, she decided she'd risk letting Larry plan and execute the party. Just thinking about him sending out invitations, getting party bags, and ordering cake put her in a sweat. I told her that was a good sign!

"I'm sure he'll mess it up," she said. "Our whole family will be embarrassed." But we came up with an expansive mind-set for the occasion to serve as an alternative focus: Learning to trust and let go is more important than a perfect party. If others judge my family negatively, I will cope. Michaela agreed to refrain from giving Larry suggestions or subtly pointing things out to him, "Even if I have to tape my mouth shut!"

At the following session Michaela proudly announced, "I was right, he blew it! But I didn't try to stop him!" Larry forgot to get party bags, and the cake he baked looked like a deflated balloon. But for Michaela, the party was a huge success. Painful as it was to watch, she didn't say a word or lift a finger to control her husband. And as a bonus, instead of scrambling to be the perfect hostess, like she normally did, she sipped a glass of wine and actually enjoyed her guests.

"I could get used to this," she joked. "And I had to admit to Larry that although it was the ugliest cake I'd ever seen, it was surprisingly delicious."

Is it hard for you to ask for help? Does it seem easier to do things yourself? Do you get annoyed when other people do things the wrong way? Would you like to be more easygoing and feel less stressed from having too much to do? Tomorrow's exercise will help you do just that.

Ask for Help **15**

Today you will ask for help with, or delegate entirely, a task you would typically do yourself. If you have a to-do list, pick an item to share or outsource. If you don't have a list, think about the tasks you usually do and choose something. At work you might ask a coworker to respond to a client, set an agenda, or lead a meeting. At home you could ask a family member to set the table, help prepare a meal, or pick something up at the grocery store. For a tougher workout, assign someone a task that you feel you are particularly good at—that you feel only you can do right.

Once you assign a job or enlist help, don't give the other person any guidance unless they specifically ask for it. If they don't do the job the way you would do it, good! You get maximum benefit from this exercise when you don't have any control over the outcome of it.

As perfectionists, all the high expectations we place on ourselves do not go away when we allow others to do something we feel responsible for. Our high expectations are merely transferred to someone else, giving us even less control over the results. Sound like a recipe for disaster? To the monkey mind it does! If the performance is "less than" by any measure, or if things aren't done "just right," it will reflect poorly on us. This might lead to rejection, or, as the monkey sees it, we'll be kicked out of the tribe. If we follow the prompting of our limbic system and try to stay in control of the task, we feed the mind-set of *It's not safe to rely on others because they can't be trusted to do it right.*

Because the monkey doesn't do risk assessment very well, it not only underestimates others' abilities, it also underestimates the cost of doing everything ourselves: feeling overwhelmed and stressed. Others often see us as "controlling," and we inadvertently make them feel bad for not doing things the way we would. And when we don't trust others with tasks, we deprive them of opportunities to develop their own way of doing things, to feel responsible, and to gain mastery.

With this exercise you'll practice trusting others to do things their own way, fostering kindness, connection, and community. And since you'll be decreasing your workload, your sense of being overwhelmed will decrease. When you refrain from correcting others or from taking over when things don't get done the way you'd like, you learn to be more flexible and forgiving. But the most valuable lesson today is realizing that you can handle it when others do things differently—even when they make mistakes. Today, you're feeding the new expansive mind-set of *I can trust other people to do things their own way, and I can trust that I can handle the consequences.*

This exercise may challenge you. Do not expect to feel trusting of your delegate. You'll likely feel anxious about how they'll perform. At the first sign of difficulty on their part, irritation, even anger, may arise. And, of course, you may fear that their less-than-perfect performance will cost you. These are normal limbic system alarms, and they don't indicate that you're a mean person! If you welcome these feelings with your breath, giving them lots of space, they'll metabolize naturally in due course.

You are going to be very tempted to correct people, point things out, and even scold others for doing something incorrectly. If you notice yourself doing any of this, congratulations! Move your self-compassion band. You can follow up with an apology and practice letting go again. If you catch yourself in time to resist the urge to control the other's performance, great! Pat yourself on the back. And every time you remind yourself of your new expansive mind-set, or remember the higher values of kindness, flexibility, and the freedom you're after, tell yourself, *Great job delegating, boss!*

Are you on the shy side? Do you tend to wait for others to start a conversation rather than initiating one yourself? Do you worry about sounding or acting foolish? Would you like to become more confident in social interactions and possibly expand your social circle? If so, tomorrow's practice is for you.

Talk to Strangers

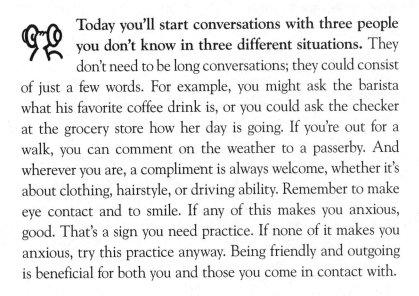

Today you'll start conversations with three people you don't know in three different situations. They don't need to be long conversations; they could consist of just a few words. For example, you might ask the barista what his favorite coffee drink is, or you could ask the checker at the grocery store how her day is going. If you're out for a walk, you can comment on the weather to a passerby. And wherever you are, a compliment is always welcome, whether it's about clothing, hairstyle, or driving ability. Remember to make eye contact and to smile. If any of this makes you anxious, good. That's a sign you need practice. If none of it makes you anxious, try this practice anyway. Being friendly and outgoing is beneficial for both you and those you come in contact with.

Perfectionists believe that to initiate a conversation, we need to have something meaningful or clever to say. If the other person doesn't respond positively to what we say, we think we've done something wrong. Awkward silences are our responsibility. Our mind-set is, *Don't risk being friendly to others, because they may not be friendly back.* As usual, the monkey mind overestimates the likelihood that our friendliness will not be reciprocated, and it underestimates our ability to recover if we annoy or bore someone.

While our health and happiness do depend, in part, on being accepted by others, adopting the unrealistic expectations of the monkey mind will not secure their acceptance. Quite the opposite. Judging ourselves this harshly, and keeping ourselves this firmly in check, further insulates and disconnects us from others.

To grow and thrive in our communities, we need to be able to make new social connections, which can lead to friendships, romantic relationships, and job opportunities. This exercise will help you gain confidence in the idea that you don't need to be perfect to make new connections with others. Being friendly, smiling, making eye contact, and starting a conversation are enough. Your new expansive mind-set is, *Initiating being friendly to others is worth the risk, and I can handle it if they are unfriendly in return.*

Of course, when we speak up, we can't expect the monkey to stay silent. From its primitive perspective, we shouldn't start a conversation unless we can be smart, witty, and confident, and since doing that is impossible with a stranger, the monkey is going to sound the fight-or-flight alarm. Since you know you're going to feel anxiety talking to strangers today, welcome it with your entire being. Just remember that if you should stumble over your words or blush, or if you cannot think of what to say to keep the conversation going, and you feel embarrassment, shame, and self-consciousness, these reactions and feelings are not a sign that you've done anything wrong. They're evidence that you are doing something right. You've stopped feeding the monkey and started moving toward your values of connection, courage, and authenticity!

If your conversation starters worked great today, and people responded to you warmly, good for you. If not, that's just as good! This exercise is designed to help you initiate connections *and* build resilience in the face of rejection. If someone doesn't respond to you the way you hoped, move your self-compassion band, praising yourself for having taken a risk. Learning to love yourself regardless of your performance or people's response to you is not the best way to build confidence in your own unique, authentic, imperfect self—it's the only way.

My husband, Doug, and I were sheltering in place during the COVID-19 crisis as I wrote this book. To help pass the time one evening, we decided to play a board game, something we only do when our children visit. We played a tile game based on strategy rather than luck. After losing to Doug four nights in a row, I remembered why we don't play games together. He's a better strategist than me, and losing leaves me feeling inadequate and angry at him—not a great way to be when you're stuck with someone for the foreseeable future. We put the game back in the box.

After a week or so my husband was pleasantly surprised when I suggested we play the game again. What he didn't know was that I'd been secretly watching online videos on winning strategies. I couldn't wait to play that night!

Then I lost again! But this time I wasn't upset; in fact, I was quite cheerful. While adopting a new playing strategy, I inadvertently adopted a new expectation about winning and losing. Since I knew learning the new strategy would take practice, I expected to struggle before getting good at it. I didn't personalize my loss, instead recognizing it as part of a learning curve. After a few more tries, I won a game! But even if I'd lost, I'd discovered that learning a new skill is very satisfying in and of itself—even more fun than winning.

Would you like to be more spontaneous and confident? Tomorrow's exercise will teach you what gets in the way of this and what to do about it.

Pick a game you've never played before, or have played but never won, and prepare to lose. If you don't have any board games, you can find games online, including traditional board games. And if you don't have an opponent handy, you can play solitaire. Whatever you play, and whoever you play with, don't play to win. Your goal is to try a strategy that you haven't used before. As long as you're playing in a new way, you're winning!

Why are we so often poor losers? Why do we get down on ourselves when someone beats us, even at a friendly board game where no money or status is involved? Thank your limbic system, which is hardwired to treat *any* loss as a potential threat to survival. If your primordial ancestor lost a fight with another tribe member, he might have lost an opportunity to attract a mate. If she were bartering for food but was outbartered by a neighbor, she might have starved. The monkey mind-set is, *Losing makes me less than others, vulnerable to rejection and death.*

But if we're unwilling to risk losing, we tend to quit at the first sign of difficulty. We avoid things we aren't already good at. And when we experience loss, which is inevitable, we feel badly about ourselves. Losing at anything, even something as low stakes as a board game, brands us, in our own imagination, as a failure.

To engage with the world more spontaneously, confidently, and skillfully, we need to get better at losing. We need to stop taking our losses personally and see them for what they are: necessary steps in the process of learning new skills. The expansive mind-set we want to cultivate is, *Losing is learning.* This exercise offers you practice using this mind-set in a low-stakes situation you can handle. When we learn to sweat the small stuff, like being willing to lose at a board game, we're better prepared for the big stuff in life. We'll be able to pursue the goals that we dream of, not just those we are good at. This is how losing makes us winners!

Since aversion to loss is hardwired into our DNA, when doing this exercise you're going to get dosed with a cocktail of uncomfortable emotions, like irritation, frustration, even embarrassment or anger. Shoulders tightening, jaw clenching, and blood pressure rising are all automatic responses preparing your body to fight an opponent. We cannot override these feelings by fighting them. Open yourself to them by rolling your shoulders and breathing slowly and deeply into your belly. This allows your discomfort to dissipate more efficiently, freeing up your mind to learn new strategies and skills.

☆ If you happen to win the game you play today, that's okay, as long as you won while in a "losing is learning" frame of mind. Your willingness to risk losing and to welcome the discomfort that losing triggers is how you get your stars. Today you're going for those values that make you a true winner—growth, openness, resilience, and self-compassion.

Do you ever feel immobilized by your to-do list? Maybe you've got so much to do that you feel overwhelmed. Which task is most important? How can you be most efficient? Should you pick the hardest one first, or should you start off easy and work your way up to it? Tomorrow's practice will help you develop more spontaneity, decrease procrastination, and increase efficiency!

Randomize Your Tasks 18

Today you will take on your to-dos in random order. Instead of making a list today, write down each thing you want to get done on an index card or small bit of paper. Next, throw them all into a hat or a bowl and, without peeking, pick one out. The to-do in your hand is the one you will take on first today. No substitutions! When you finish the task, draw another in the same random fashion, and so on. If outside events make any task too difficult, put the to-do back in the hat and draw again. One caveat: don't include time-sensitive tasks, such as your dentist appointment or picking up the kids after school!

A surgeon once confided to me that he always took a list of the correct steps for a procedure to the operating room. Even if he had performed the operation a hundred times, he had a nurse check his actions against the list. He told me that being human, he was bound to make mistakes, and using a list to help prevent mistakes gave him peace of mind.

As perfectionists, we often approach life as if it were an operating room where someone's life depends on us doing things in a perfect sequence. Our monkey mind-set is, *If I don't do things in the correct order, something bad will happen.* Imposing this expectation on ourselves can turn even the simplest to-do list into a stressful agenda. When we run into obstacles, instead of being flexible, we get frustrated. We expect others to comply with our plans and try to control their behavior. We try to multitask so we don't fall behind. Or, if our first to-do is too difficult to perform correctly, we may put off our to-dos altogether.

☀ Because I'm a planner by nature, this is one of my personal go-to exercises, as well as a favorite when working with clients. I keep a supply of index cards on hand, and my desk drawer is filled with to-do cards ready to be recycled when the task needs to be done again. The expansive mind-set for this practice is, *It is okay to do things out of order. I'll still be getting something done!*

Giving up control of the order in which we accomplish our to-dos creates several shifts in the perfectionist. It forces us to be flexible, encouraging spontaneity. Removing a task from the context of a list increases our awareness of the task, encouraging mindful focus on what we're doing instead of on what remains to be done. And if you sometimes procrastinate with tasks, addressing them at random makes it easier to get started. These combined benefits can even make us more productive than we would be using a list.

🕸 Freeing yourself from rigid self-imposed order isn't easy. You may feel like things are getting out of control, which can be quite painful. If you pick an insignificant task first, you may feel anxious that you're wasting precious time. If you pick a difficult one you may feel overwhelmed. You may get annoyed at a task that you didn't want to do just then, or disappointed that you didn't pick the task you feel like doing. If the order you wind up doing things doesn't feel efficient, you may get anxious about whether you'll get all your tasks done. These emotions are natural and necessary growing pains for the change you're creating. So welcome them, bringing your attention to your breath, and continue with the exercise. You're teaching your limbic system to be more relaxed and easygoing, no matter what needs to be done.

⭐ If you happen to pick the task that you wanted to do first, it's okay, but it's not a cause for celebration. The more uncomfortable you are with this exercise, the more you'll grow from it. For example, if you end up driving into town twice, instead of once, because you did things out of order, don't kick yourself for your inefficiency. Instead, pat yourself on the back or move your self-compassion band, gently reminding yourself that inefficiency is part of the exercise. You're learning that you can survive, even thrive, outside of your comfort zone.

My husband, Doug, and I attended a weeklong workshop a few years ago led by a husband-and-wife team. While both were unpretentious, Steve was exceptionally casual about his appearance. His hair expressed itself in such comical ways that I wondered whether he ever bothered to look in the bathroom mirror. Then, midway through the week, he topped himself. As he bade us all good morning with his usual grin, there was a noticeable black space where there had been a front tooth. With his disheveled hair, faded Hawaiian shirt, wrinkled cargo shorts, and flip-flops—and now a gap in his teeth—he looked like a goofball, not someone you could take seriously.

I waited for an explanation, but it didn't come. For the next couple of hours Steve commenced to do his usual thing: amazing heart-opening teaching that commanded the attention and devotion of the class. It wasn't until the afternoon session that his wife suggested he explain the missing tooth. In light of the lesson he'd taught me, the explanation was unnecessary. It is possible, I realized, to be so unselfconscious and possess such confidence, that one's appearance simply doesn't matter. I marveled to myself, What freedom that must allow!

Do you feel insecure about your appearance? Obsess over perceived flaws? Would you like to think less about how you look and instead feel more confident? If you answer yes, tomorrow's exercise is for you.

Show Your Rough Edges **19**

Today, notice every time you check your appearance for flaws. Then tomorrow, see how many "appearance checks" you can eliminate. The first day of this two-day exercise is a mindfulness practice, focusing your attention on your behavior without attempting to judge or change it. How much time and energy do you spend grooming in front of the mirror, stepping on the scale, inspecting your body, choosing clothing, and asking others, "How do I look?" (To help you keep track, there's a Body-Checking Form available for download at http://monkeymindbooks.com/p/.) It may surprise you how often you check your appearance in store windows, car mirrors, and the eyes of others. And yes, checking your phone camera in selfie mode counts!

On the second day, having more awareness of these behaviors, you can begin to curb some of your urges. How much you reduce this checking behavior is up to you, but I suggest you cut the obvious things, like mirror and scale checking, in half. See if you can completely refrain from asking others how you look or touching parts of your body you feel insecure about. Don't camouflage what you think are your flaws. For example, I often blush when I'm nervous, and I used to wear a scarf or turtleneck to cover it. Now, if I'm giving a presentation, I wear scoop-necked shirts and no scarf.

It is natural, of course, to care about how we look. As individuals, we need to attract a mate to procreate, which, collectively, ensures the survival of our species. Our limbic system is hardwired to stop us from going out into the world looking like we just fell out of bed. Add to that a beauty product industry that rakes in hundreds of millions a year and inundates us with advertising featuring impossibly beautiful models, it's no wonder so many of us believe, *I can only be happy, loved, and worthwhile if there are no flaws in my appearance.* This monkey mind-set keeps us in a perpetual state of stress, contributing to eating disorders, anxiety, and depression.

This exercise is designed to help you learn to feel good about yourself without the condition that you look attractive to others. The expansive mind-set you'll cultivate is, *My worth is not dependent on my appearance.* Note that I said "cultivate." If you are a perfectionist about your figure, grooming, wardrobe, or all of the above, the idea that you could be happy with yourself unconditionally, without looking your best, may sound impossible. But with new experiences, our beliefs can change. Today you'll acquire the new experience of *not knowing how you look.* If you're willing to try this exercise, you'll be surprised to discover not only how little our rough edges matter to others, but how much freedom is found in not needing to check your appearance.

Every glance in the mirror, smoothing out of the wrinkles in our clothes, or checking of lipstick is a reaction to an alert from the monkey mind: *Woo-woo-woo! Something is wrong!* And the more we check, the more we affirm for the monkey that our appearance *needs* to be checked. To become comfortable with our occasionally less-than-perfect appearance, we must stop feeding the monkey with this checking behavior. You'll feel more insecure and anxious in the short run, but hang in there! Breathe into your discomfort, and place your hand on your heart. Know that you are okay just as you are.

Did you use your self-compassion band and praise yourself profusely when you resisted an urge to check? You get stars for that. And of course, the more urges you resist, the more stars you earn. And when you give in to an urge and are kind to yourself, give yourself a bonus star for practicing self-compassion.

Does it take you a long time to get things done because you check and double-check your work to make sure you didn't make a mistake? Tomorrow's exercise will increase your work efficiency and help you gain confidence in yourself.

Pick a task, and then complete it without stopping to evaluate your progress or the quality of your work. If you're writing a report or an email, let the first draft be the final draft. If you're mopping the floor, don't look to see if you missed a spot. Dress without trying different things on or asking anybody how you look. Once you begin the task, just forge ahead without checking and rechecking for mistakes. Keep moving forward and don't look back.

As perfectionists, we believe that making a mistake will lead to a catastrophic outcome. We assume that others will judge us as incompetent and we'll lose respect. Our mind-set is, *I must do things perfectly, or I have failed.* The cost of this mind-set is high. We double- and triple-check everything we do, so we don't have time or energy left for self-care, or to strike a balance between work and play. Because our sense of self-worth depends so much on eliminating errors, we have high levels of stress and anxiety. And because our performance seldom matches the expectations we have for ourselves, we can suffer from depression.

The expansive mind-set you want to adopt today is, *Making a mistake means I'm human, not that I'm incompetent.* As reasonable as this sounds, the only way you'll begin to believe it is by allowing yourself to make mistakes, and then dealing with the consequences. Over time you'll learn that the mistakes you make are not as catastrophic as the monkey mind would have you believe. If you can forgive and accept yourself—foibles and all—you'll be less stressed, more relaxed, and less susceptible to depression. And since you're not stopping to evaluate yourself constantly, you'll have more time for relationships and other interests.

Allowing mistakes is new territory for you; you're going to feel uncomfortable. Imagine how early explorers felt while sailing toward what looked like the edge of the earth. To prove that the world was round, they had to risk dropping off the edge. Be an explorer today. Instead of retreating to your familiar habit of mistake-proofing your work, keep moving forward toward your edge and don't look back. Breathe deep, and allow the anxiety to be while reminding yourself of what you're after. Freed from unrealistic expectations, you can not only get things done more efficiently, you can also discover the feeling of flow in your life.

Don't let the monkey evaluate your work. This part of your brain will howl when your performance is less than perfect. Instead, cheer for yourself for taking a risk and venturing into new territory. Use your self-compassion band to remind yourself that imperfectly done tasks simply make you human. Instead of perfect work, you're after the better and bigger goal of unconditional self-acceptance. It will take commitment and perseverance, but by repeating this exercise you can achieve it!

Lindsey came to her session with a dilemma. A dear friend whose father had recently passed away had asked her to come for a visit, but on the same weekend she was signed up for a seminar offered once a year. Lindsey felt conflicted. Missing the seminar would be a big disappointment, but she wanted to support her friend. She looked at me, hoping I would help her make the right decision, so I guided her through a decision-making exercise.

First, I had Lindsey write down pros and cons for each option. Then I asked her to assign a numerical importance to each pro and con on a scale of 1 to 3, with 1 being sort of important, 2 important, and 3 very important. For example, she rated the pro "I won't have to wait until next year" as a 2. She rated the con "I would be letting my friend down" as a 3. When she was finished, she added up her two columns and looked at me with surprise.

"The totals match almost exactly!" she said. I wasn't surprised. This happened nearly every time I did this exercise with clients. If there is a significant imbalance between the pros and cons of anything we're comparing, we'd have an easier choice to make.

Lindsey's expression darkened. "This doesn't really help me. No matter what I do I'll have to give up something." She sounded frustrated and discouraged, but she was making great progress. She was beginning to understand the inherent imperfection in any choice we make.

Does the fear of making the wrong decision sometime paralyze you with fear? Tomorrow you'll learn to be both decisive and confident.

21 Decide and Conquer

Today you will make a decision without being certain whether you're making the perfect choice. Sound unwise? The truth is, trying to make perfect decisions is the leading cause of not making decisions and suffering unnecessarily once we do. If you often get stuck trying to choose correctly, this is the exercise for you. There are four steps, but if you reach a decision after the first or the second, you can skip the remaining steps.

1. Set a timer for two to five minutes, depending on how complex your decision is. Write down all the pros and cons you can think of for each choice. Stop when the time is up.

2. Assign a numerical importance to each pro and con on a scale of 1 to 3: 1 = sort of important, 2 = important, 3 = very important. Then add up the columns.

3. Set the timer for one minute. Review the pros and cons, or go with your gut, but when the timer goes off, make your decision.

4. If you still haven't decided, flip a coin.

Even though this exercise can be done with multiple choices, for your first time keep it simple. The dilemma you choose should be an either/or choice between two things. It's also best to start with a low-stakes decision, like whether to eat out or in. The exercise will trigger discomfort, and you should work out at a level that won't overwhelm you. But with practice, you'll find this method works for big decisions too.

What makes this simple exercise challenging is that, as perfectionists, we believe there is a "right" decision, and if we make a "wrong" choice we've failed and deserve to be punished. Some decisions are that straightforward; for example, deciding to run a red light may get you a ticket. But most decisions are more complex, with lots of pros and cons to reconcile. Unlike our executive brain, which is well equipped to work with complexity, for the monkey mind the only allowable decision is a perfect one, meaning an outcome with zero negative consequences. But no amount of research, thought, or worry will accomplish that. To reach any decision at all, we must conquer the monkey mind-set that says, *Any choice that has a downside is wrong, and if I make a wrong decision I'm a fool!*

In a world with no perfect choices, our only choice is to learn to live expansively with our decisions, no matter what the result. Today you'll embrace the expansive mind-set of *Any decision I take responsibility for and grow from is the right decision.* When a decision turns out favorably, you can exercise gratitude and open up to joy. When a decision turns out poorly, you can exercise self-compassion, get creative, and build resilience. The more decisions you make, the more opportunities you'll have to honor your true values, rather than the monkey's.

Over time, you'll become more comfortable with risk and grow more confident that you can handle the consequences of any decision you make.

There will be plenty of emotions to welcome in this exercise. When you survey your list of pros and cons, you may feel confused, even desperate, spinning your wheels trying to resolve them. Since any choice will have a downside, you're going to feel a measure of apprehension or fear when making it. You may also feel irritability and resentment for having to decide, and if it's a decision you've been putting off, you might feel shame for not having yet decided. These emotions are here to visit, not to stay. Focus your attention on your breath flowing in and out. Welcome what you're feeling.

First of all, if you made *any* decision, congratulations! If your decision worked out well for you, that's good. If it didn't, that's good too. Your intention is to practice decisiveness and self-compassion, not to make perfect choices. Each time you welcome your feelings while following through with your decision, or remind yourself of your expansive mind-set, move your self-compassion band or give yourself a pat on the back, or do both. You deserve it!

If you need information or help, do you sometimes do without rather than risk the chance of being refused? Tomorrow's exercise will help you develop the strength to handle those dreaded nos.

22 Go for the No

Today you will purposely ask for things while expecting no for an answer. That's right. You're going to be refused, denied, and rejected—*on purpose!* Because we're so conditioned to make only reasonable requests of others, it may take a little work to imagine yourself doing this exercise. Consider starting off by asking your significant other for a back rub while they're getting ready to go to work. Or you might ask a stranger on the subway for a stick of gum or a breath mint, the barista for a discount on your latte, or a police officer if they'll take a selfie with you. Or try ordering something not on the menu at a restaurant.

Three don'ts to note: Don't make intrusive or personal requests; the purpose of this exercise is to make you uncomfortable, not the person you're asking. Don't ask for something you're not prepared to accept if you get a yes. And if you do get a yes, don't remain satisfied with that. Keep asking for things until you get a no. Remember, as is true with all the exercises in this book, you can start out small and work your way up to more challenging refusals.

While this exercise may sound like a fool's errand, it's a clever way to confront perfectionism. It puts us face-to-face with the biggest fear we have other than death itself: rejection. Our unconscious monkey mind-set is, *Any rejection is*

dangerous because it can lead to me being kicked out of my tribe.
Hijacked by this way of thinking, we're unable go after what we
truly want and need because we're not willing to risk rejection.
And our sense of self-worth remains fragile, as it's overly dependent on others' approval.

As you experience being told no, you'll begin to recognize that rejection is not as catastrophic as you think.
As you gain confidence that you can handle it, you're more
likely to go after the things you want. Professionally, you may
risk going for a promotion, or ask for a raise, or invest in your
own business idea. Socially, you may initiate more friendships,
go on more dates, or lead and inspire others. Personally, you
won't be so hesitant about asking for what you want, and you'll
develop a sturdier sense of your own worth. The expansive
mind-set that you'll be feeding is, *Rejection is not dangerous; I
can handle it and take more risks in life.* And with each refusal,
denial, and rejection you receive, you'll come closer to believing this.

Asking for a no takes a lot of courage; you're exposing
yourself to primordial fear. You're likely to feel highly
anxious anticipating the exercise, and you'll probably feel
embarrassment, even shame, when you're refused. But expo-
sure to these emotions is the most direct way to learn resilience, and resilience is what will free you. You can build
resilience with your welcoming breath, opening and creating
space for these emotions to come and go.

Be extra kind and supportive toward yourself today. Don't leave the house without your self-compassion band; it will serve as a reminder of what you're after and as an acknowledgment when you get the no. Remember that negative feelings are a sign that you're getting a lot out of the exercise. If you're not sweating, you are not getting stronger, so sweat, shake, blush!

⭐ If you embarrassed yourself today, congratulations! Tell yourself how brave you are and move your self-compassion band. If you maintained your dignity today, ask yourself whether you truly took a risk. Remember that getting a thumbs-down from others is how you give yourself a thumbs-up! Try again tomorrow; you can "go for the no" anytime you are so inspired!

To fulfill a foreign language requirement in the tenth grade, I chose German. Even though it wasn't my first choice, I fell in love with German and stuck with it all through high school and college. In my junior year in college I enrolled in a six-month study-abroad program in Germany. I had performed well in my classes and was confident in my abilities, and I was excited about all the people I'd connect with and the culture I'd absorb.

But the native Germans spoke much more quickly than I was used to. It was difficult to grasp what they were saying. My responses were sometimes met with blank stares. Once a group of younger girls asked me for the time, and when I transposed the numbers they laughed out loud at me. I was so sensitive to being judged that I began avoiding conversing with native Germans, instead speaking mostly to other students in my language classes. Of course, my fluency and confidence didn't improve. I developed few connections with the people or the culture of the country. When I returned to the United States, I stopped speaking German entirely.

Do you worry about how smart and coherent you sound? Do you avoid using words and phrases that you haven't used before? When someone doesn't understand you correctly, do you automatically blame yourself? Do you sometimes stay silent rather than risk embarrassing yourself with something you say? Tomorrow's exercise will give you some great practice overcoming the shame and embarrassment that can arise in conversation.

23 Butcher a Word or Phrase

Today you will intentionally mispronounce a word or misuse a phrase. When it comes to verbal communication, we all get it wrong sometimes. Today you're going to purposely get it wrong. You could go to a coffee shop and order a "laddie" instead of a "latte." At a restaurant ask for a "scissors salad" instead of a "Caesar salad." Or, say the straight route between two locations is "as the cow flies." Plan in advance when and where you're going to do your butchering; however, if you should happen across an unexpected opportunity to say it wrong, *squeeze* the moment!

Don't offer an apology or explanation, such as "Sorry, I misspoke!" Just let the mistake you've made be there. Whatever happens, you can handle it.

While we hear others mispronouncing words all the time, and think nothing of it, when we do it ourselves, we make excuses and beat ourselves up. As perfectionists, on an unconscious level we hold ourselves to a higher standard. That's because everything we say is being carefully monitored by the monkey mind, which has a very low tolerance of risk. To the monkey, mispronouncing a word or phrase reveals our ignorance. We could lose others' respect and wind up discredited and excluded from society—an existential threat. When we think with the monkey, our mind-set is, *I cannot handle appearing foolish and possibly being judged by others; it's too risky.*

When we think we must appear knowledgeable so as not to appear foolish, we're likely to avoid conversations about subjects we're unfamiliar with, or with unfamiliar people and in unfamiliar situations. This isn't how we learn and grow. When our sense of worth is dependent on others thinking we're always fluent and smart, our self-esteem is very fragile. To become more knowledgeable and self-secure, we must be willing to appear foolish. The expansive mind-set we need is, *It is okay to appear foolish to others. I can handle it!* This is how we feed our own higher values—authenticity, vulnerability, and curiosity—and not the monkey.

The only way we can get comfortable with the possibility of being judged by others is to expose ourselves to potential judgment. This exercise will do that. It will make you anxious and bring up challenging emotions like shame and embarrassment, the fight-or-flight alarms delivered by your limbic system. Remember whose hairy finger is on that alarm button! Welcome these emotions with open arms; they are proof that you are growing. Over time, they will diminish. Use your self-compassion band to praise yourself for your courage, reminding yourself of your expansive mind-set. By exercising self-compassion you're building a more solid, secure foundation of self-worth.

☆ When you butcher a word or phrase today, results will differ. If others correct you, and you take the correction gracefully, good job! Give yourself a pat on the back! If you made an excuse for it, or revealed that it was an intentional mistake, good job noticing! Move your self-compassion band and forgive yourself. There are plenty of words and phrases just waiting for a good hatchet job tomorrow!

Do you beat yourself up when you fail at something or don't perform up to your own expectations? Would you like to be more loving and compassionate with yourself? Tomorrow's exercise will help you do just that!

24 Fail and Forgive

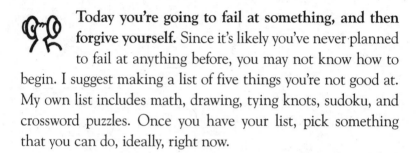

Today you're going to fail at something, and then forgive yourself. Since it's likely you've never planned to fail at anything before, you may not know how to begin. I suggest making a list of five things you're not good at. My own list includes math, drawing, tying knots, sudoku, and crossword puzzles. Once you have your list, pick something that you can do, ideally, right now.

All humans are averse to failure. Our earliest ancestors may not have had a word for it, but when they returned home from a hunting or gathering expedition empty-handed, they felt shame. Our limbic system is hardwired to prevent failure.

Though we've evolved to understand that making mistakes and falling short of goals is necessary for learning, our limbic system has not. The monkey mind-set is, *Failing at what I set out to do means I am not good enough.* Making success a prerequisite for having good self-esteem is a tough standard to live by. When we cannot meet this standard, we criticize and punish ourselves, imagining our shame will somehow improve us. When it doesn't, we limit our activity to what we can do well. We can't learn new skills if we can't risk failure.

When we go after what we truly want, we will fall, make mistakes, and be awkward and clumsy. The mind-set we perfectionists need is one of self-compassion: *Failing means I have taken a risk, and risk-taking is how I learn.* Our intention must be to forgive rather than to rebuke ourselves when we fail to meet the high expectations we have for ourselves. This will allow us to regain our footing and keep moving forward.

Of course, we may know intellectually that encouragement works better than ridicule, but it's hard to uproot the perfectionist beliefs we've had our whole life. Self-compassion, like any skill, needs to be practiced. When you fail at something, talk to yourself as you would a young child. Here are some affirmations to add to your expansive mind-set. Repeat them to yourself again and again. You can't overuse them!

It is okay to "fail."

I am proud of myself for trying something I'm not good at.

Keep going; I don't have to be good at this.

I'm doing a great job trying something I'm not naturally good at.

When you fail to perform as well as you'd like, or as well as you imagine others would, you'll likely feel frustration, shame, even anger. This is a good sign. It means you are fully engaged in the exercise and that your perfectionistic tendencies have been activated. When you feel these emotions, don't give in to the urge to try harder. Instead, practice breathing into them, and remind yourself of your expansive mind-set. The more welcoming you are to the feeling of failure, the better your body will be at processing it, and the less influence it will have on you in your life. And remember that the space you're expanding to make room for these uncomfortable feelings is the same space in which more patience, kindness, and forgiveness will flourish. Not only can you offer yourself these components of compassion, but you can give them to others as well!

☆ It may be harder to intentionally fail than you think. If you accidentally pick something that you wound up succeeding at, then pick something more challenging to try next time. But if you did manage to make a mistake, misunderstand a direction, not finish what you started, or somehow muck things up, great! Massive failure deserves massive stars. Move your self-compassion band, give yourself a pat on the back, and tell yourself, *Good job!*

This morning, while writing the following exercise, I decided I needed a break and headed to the gym. While I was lacing up my tennis shoes in the locker room, a woman reached for her towel lying next to me on the bench. "Oh, sorry!" I blurted out, for possibly being in her way. Realizing how absurd and unnecessary my apology was, I laughed and confided that I had just written about that very thing this morning. She laughed, too, and told me she'd been working on her own apologetic tendencies for years!

While riding my bike home after my workout, I came up behind three women walking abreast and rang my bell to alert them. When they repositioned themselves to make way for me, I noticed my discomfort at disrupting their walk, and I had a strong urge to offer them a "Sorry!" as I passed. Instead I said, "Thanks!" That felt uncomfortable too. Would they see me as entitled? For me, learning how to take up space in the world—without apologizing for it—is an ongoing project!

Have you ever been told that you apologize too much? Have you ever wondered this yourself? Do excuses pop out of your mouth before anyone questions you? In tomorrow's exercise you'll take a close look at how and when you feel the need to apologize.

25 Mind Your Apologies

Today, you'll notice every time you excuse yourself or apologize for anything to anyone. For example, you might reach for the coffeepot at the same moment as someone else and say, "Sorry!" You might apologize for accidentally interrupting someone, or you might forget someone's name and make a joke about how you're getting senile. Or maybe you'll answer an email and begin with the phrase, "Sorry for the delay." You might even catch yourself making an excuse for the food you prepare for guests tonight: "It would be better if I'd marinated it longer." Any time you apologize for anything you do or fail to do today, whether it's an inconsequential mistake or a near fatal error, take note.

Don't try to curtail your excuses or apologies. Today's is a mindfulness exercise; you're simply observing what is for most of us unconscious behavior. At the website for this book, you can download a tally sheet to help you keep track of what you observe.

Apologies and excuses are important components of social intercourse. They show others that we take responsibility for our actions and communicate that we care about their feelings. But when we reflexively apologize or make an excuse without awareness or intention, we're likely reacting out of fear, hijacked by the monkey mind. To the monkey, anything that falls short of perfect, no matter how small—like simply being in someone else's way—subjects us to the judgment of others. Apologizing or making an excuse shows that we've already judged ourselves. This preemptive behavior is meant to ward off attacks. Our monkey mind-set is, *The best defense is a good offense. Don't leave room for anyone to judge you.* When you observe yourself apologizing today, see if you notice this kind of thinking.

If you can, also take note of how people respond to your apologies and excuses. Does apologizing encourage or discourage others from criticizing you? Are others quick to forgive and reassure? Do they sometimes reply with an apology of their own?

☀ Since your apologies and excuses are unconscious judgments you've made of yourself, making yourself aware of them can provoke more judgment and test your self-compassion. We don't need to make excuses for our excuses! The expansive mind-set you want to embrace today is, *Apologizing isn't wrong or right. It's part of the perfectly imperfect me.* What you're practicing today is unconditional acceptance of whatever is happening in this moment, including what you may suspect is unnecessary excuse making.

Be aware that any extra scrutiny we give our mistakes, or our excuses for them, will trigger negative emotions. Mindful self-awareness is tough to maintain when we're feeling shame, embarrassment, or discouragement. Whatever feelings and sensations that arise are to be welcomed. They're just something else to notice. You'll find a place to note them on your tally sheet.

Every time you notice yourself making an excuse or an apology, reward that observation by moving your self-compassion band. Every time you take the time to note what you've noticed on the tally sheet, give yourself a pat on the back or on the heart. At the end of your day, when you've reviewed your tally, tell yourself, *Good work!* And if you didn't keep tally, or you were unable to catch yourself in the act, no apology necessary! Just have another go of it tomorrow.

Do you find yourself making excuses and apologizing all the time? Tomorrow's exercise will help you develop self-acceptance and self-confidence.

26 Make No Excuses

Today, you'll resist the urge to apologize or make excuses for yourself or your behavior and instead **"own it."** If you arrive late to work and want to blame the traffic or the line at the coffee shop, you'll remain quiet, say "hello" to the boss, and get to work. If you're leading a meeting, you won't first explain how you didn't have time to adequately prepare an agenda. You'll say how hard you worked on it. And if you arrive at a doorway at the same time as someone else, and you both stop short to avoid a collision, instead of saying, "Sorry!" you'll thank the person for letting you go first. In all the situations you might reflexively offer an excuse or an apology for yourself, you'll practice self-acceptance instead.

This exercise is a follow-up to the preceding exercise, in which you observed and tracked your apologetic and excuse-making behavior throughout the day, so please do that one first. Building awareness of the types of situations that invoke these habits prepares you to know what to expect, so the urges will be less likely to blindside you.

While excusing ourselves and apologizing for behavior is sometimes necessary, perfectionists feel the need to apologize if there's the slightest chance we've offended someone.

Any failure to meet another's expectations requires an excuse. Every move we make must please not only us, but anyone who might conceivably be judging us.

Unfortunately, the monkey mind in charge of our limbic system is not good at risk assessment. It perceives even our most inconsequential imperfections as grounds for rejection by others, and then prompts us to *Do something about it!* By apologizing for ourselves, we make it unnecessary for others to criticize us. Our excuses preempt others' judgments. The monkey mind-set we adopt is, *If I acknowledge my failure first, or explain it somehow, others won't judge me for it.*

Any safety that unwarranted excuses and apologies bring comes at a cost. Excuses and apologies encourage others to reassure us, rather than give us honest feedback we can learn from. And they send a message to the monkey mind that excuses and apologies *are* necessary, even for the smallest, most inconsequential failings. They are food for the monkey, which means more unwarranted fight-or-flight feelings in the future for our inconsequential mistakes.

The expansive mind-set you're building today is, *I don't need to defend myself for making mistakes or inconveniencing others. I can handle others' judgments.* This way of thinking and acting not only tames the monkey, it reinforces the belief that we have a right to take up room in the world. And, because not making excuses or apologies forces us to own our shortcomings, we have an opportunity to practice forgiving ourselves, whether or not we imagine anybody else does. Self-compassion is the essential ingredient to the self-confidence we all long to feel.

Without the protection that you think excuses give you, you're sure to feel more anxiety about being criticized. Thanking someone for accommodating you, instead of apologizing, may cause you embarrassment. Anxiety and embarrassment are the monkey mind's call to action to defend yourself. Instead of acting on these feelings, make room for them with your welcoming breath. They are the inevitable growing pains of learning to accept yourself and your rightful place on earth. The more painful emotions you welcome, the more you are growing.

Don't give yourself a hard time when the word "sorry" escapes your lips before you catch it. Apologizing and making excuses are deeply ingrained habits, and it takes time to change them. Give yourself a pat on the back for noticing, or move your self-compassion band, and be patient. Ultimately, today's is an exercise in self-compassion, not just mastery over excuse making and unnecessary apologies.

I'm one of those people who loves doing laundry. The smell of the clean clothes, the heat while taking them out of the dryer, and the folding all feel very satisfying, as does the sense of accomplishment I feel for getting a little task done. But one thing I never learned was how to fold a fitted sheet. Then, a few months ago, I found a two-minute online video that promised to teach me in four simple steps.

But thirty seconds in, I was floundering. Just hold the two corners of the sheet lengthwise with the right side facing me. Ummmm, okay. Next, take the long end and fold the right corner over the left—Huh?—then down the width of the sheet and fold the third corner into the two already folded corners. What? And damn, this instructor moves fast for a lady my age! *I watched the video eight times, and I still didn't have a clue.* Argh!

I found another video with the same simple promise. I watched it six times and still could not do it. I tried a third video. Still baffled. Desperate, I returned to the first one. But I was still mystified, and my frustration was building. I had thought this fun project would take thirty minutes tops, and then I would have lunch. But I was too stubborn to quit.

Finally, after an hour the heavens opened, the lightning struck, and in my trembling hands I held a nearly perfectly folded freaking fitted sheet! Exhausted and irritable, I went downstairs and had lunch. As my headache receded and my blood sugar returned to normal, I wondered, How did I manage to turn something that was supposed to be fun into such a stressful experience?

I retraced my steps. (No, not the steps to fold a fitted sheet. I probably wouldn't be able to replicate those!) How did I approach the task? Well, I assumed I'd master the folding of fitted sheets right away, that I wouldn't make any mistakes. I decided that the next time I wanted to learn something, I'd bring the spirit of a genius teacher along. As Albert Einstein is reported to have said, "Anyone who has never made a mistake has never tried anything new."

Do you tend to avoid things you don't know how to do, and stick to what you're good at? Do you feel envious of other people who have fun hobbies and fulfilling interests? Do you ever miss out on career advancements because you lack confidence in your ability to learn necessary new skills? Then this next exercise is for you.

Be a Newbie

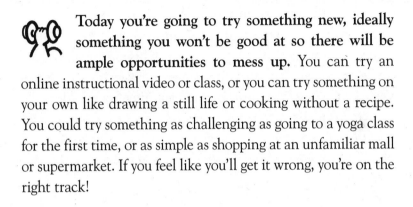 Today you're going to try something new, ideally something you won't be good at so there will be ample opportunities to mess up. You can try an online instructional video or class, or you can try something on your own like drawing a still life or cooking without a recipe. You could try something as challenging as going to a yoga class for the first time, or as simple as shopping at an unfamiliar mall or supermarket. If you feel like you'll get it wrong, you're on the right track!

A sure sign of perfectionism is the belief that mistakes are a sign of weakness. Compared to others who are performing flawlessly, we feel we are less worthy as human beings. This harsh perspective reflects the survival agenda of the limbic system, which correctly observes that mastery of tasks increases our chances of survival. So, using monkey logic, it equates mistakes with failure. But the monkey mind doesn't understand that repeated trial and error is the only path to mastery. This lack of insight has a great cost. When our executive brain gets hijacked, and we see mistakes as a failing, we cannot be open to trying new things. We live narrow, constricted lives devoid of risks and the rewards that risks can deliver. The mind-set we live by is, *To be safe and worthy, I must not make a mistake.*

This exercise will teach you to take a different stance toward mistakes. The expansive mind-set you're reinforcing is, *Making a mistake is a sign that I have taken a risk by trying something new and is an opportunity for growth.* You'll be exercising this mind-set in a low-stakes planned situation today, but if you practice repeatedly, over time you'll be more willing to try new things, more open to the risk of making a mistake, and more forgiving of yourself when you make a mistake. Since you'll be making more mistakes, and learning from them, you'll gain more mastery in more areas of your life. And because you'll by cultivating self-compassion for your mistakes instead of self-punishment, you will develop a more solid sense of your own worthiness.

Although you'll be changing your behavior and adopting a new way of thinking, you can expect that your emotions won't change. You're bound to feel apprehension and anxiety about the new thing you're trying, and at the first obstacle to progress you'll likely feel frustration or embarrassment, or both. And if you *do* mess up, you're going to feel ashamed. All these emotions are normal and to be expected. Your intention today is to keep breathing and give them however much time they need to play out. They can't last forever, especially when you no longer feed them your old, unconscious "mistakes = failure" beliefs.

☆ When we make a mistake, our reflex is to kick ourselves. Today you're learning to pat yourself on the back instead. It's okay if you don't catch your reflex in time to stop it. Just give yourself two pats on the back, once for noticing your old self-punishing ways, and again for having made a mistake. And don't forget your self-compassion band. It's an excellent visual reminder to praise yourself for your mistakes.

Do you get stressed and overwhelmed by all that you have to do? When you start something, is it hard to stop until the task is complete, even if you end up feeling depleted? Would you like to feel more relaxed and easygoing and have more energy? If so, then tomorrow's exercise is for you.

Stop in the Name of Love

Today you'll stop working on a task before it is complete. You'll choose something you normally wouldn't stop doing until it was done. Maybe you'll do half the dishes and leave the rest. Maybe you'll leave the office with email unanswered or a report not turned in. Maybe you'll vacuum just one floor of the house, or leave one of your errands undone. It doesn't matter what task you pick as long as it isn't time sensitive or doesn't directly affect others.

Most perfectionists can only rest and relax once everything is done. This strategy originated with our primal drive to secure food and shelter, without which we'd have been vulnerable to famine, the weather, and predators. The monkey mind-set is, *I can only rest when every task is completed.*

It's fine to get things done, but if we must get everything done to feel fine, we have a problem. In our busy lives, there will always be something else deserving of our attention. We hop from task to task in a fight-or-flight frenzy, never stopping to rest and relax. By day's end we're stressed out and overwhelmed, and our mind and body are stuck in a tightly wound state. When we don't make time for self-care and self-compassion, we live productive, but joyless, lives.

The expansive mind-set we want to cultivate is, *Self-care is just as essential to my safety and well-being as is taking care of business.* Allowing ourselves time to rejuvenate will make us stronger in everything we do. We may discover that there is pleasure in doing things, not just in getting them done. And when we allow ourselves to rest when we need to, instead of when we think we deserve to, we'll have much more energy to devote to other aspects of life, like our relationships and creative projects. Taking our attention away from "getting things done" will make us more easygoing, less controlling, and potentially more pleasant to be around. This is what I mean by *stopping in the name of love!*

Leaving something undone won't be easy; you are likely to experience frustration, insecurity, and anxiety. These feelings are the call to action of the monkey mind, which we don't want to feed. Breathe in slowly and deeply, allowing your emotions to play out. Don't give in to the urge to return to the task.

When you welcome the punishing emotions that leaving something undone can generate, you deserve lots of praise and encouragement. Give yourself a star or two, move your self-compassion band, and tell yourself silently, or better yet out loud, *I am learning to let go. Good for me! This is hard, but I can do it.* And remember, the more often you repeat your expansive mind-set, the better your workout, and the more stars you get.

Think you're not creative? Would you like to be more spontaneous and willing to take more risks? Tomorrow's practice will
help with all of the above.

29 Be a Real Artist

Grab some markers! Get out your children's art supplies! Today you're going to be an artist. That's right. You're going to draw, scribble, or paint. Any medium you have around the house—pencils, colored pens, watercolors, even finger paints—will do, but if you're inspired to go to an art store, do it!

Allocate at least five minutes for this exercise, but you can spend as long as you like on it. You can start with a drawing prompt, such as a waterfall, a tree, or the sun, or take an abstract approach. If you feel blocked, just scribble for a while. Should you happen to have some drawing skill or experience, challenge yourself by using your nondominant hand. If your creativity doesn't flow, that's okay. Just keep scribbling.

Producing something that will satisfy the critics is not the purpose of this exercise. You simply want to experience the process of facing a blank sheet of paper and of expressing yourself.

As children, we were blissfully absorbed with our crayons and coloring books, but as adults, most of us feel uncomfortable doing anything with a pen other than signing our name. At a certain point in our lives, or perhaps gradually over the years, we adopted the monkey mind-set of *If I can't draw well, I shouldn't be drawing at all.* The possibility of our work being judged is too big a risk, and even if there's nobody around, our biggest critic, the monkey, is always with us.

As you draw or paint, notice what judgments arise. Every time you notice self-criticism, remind yourself that it's coming from your frightened monkey mind. Redirect yourself to your new expansive mind-set: *Taking a creative risk, no matter the result, is always good enough.* If you can accept risk this way, you can allow yourself to become completely absorbed and focused on what you're doing—what is known as a "flow state." Is there any better way to live?

Of course, strong feelings of shame, insecurity, confusion, and irritation will accompany those judgmental thoughts. Even professional artists experience this. Keep breathing with an awareness of the inner space you are creating—a blank canvas upon which your painful feelings can express themselves. Eventually their colors will fade, making way for new brushstrokes of spontaneity and joy.

You'll be tempted to look at your artwork and compare it to what someone with talent might produce. Thank the monkey for its opinion and remember that you're not after rave reviews. If you expressed yourself, no matter how clumsily, and left a mark, no matter how illegible, you're a real artist today!

About ten years ago I visited my oldest girlfriend. I was eager to tell her all about my latest passion: working on my perfectionism. She'd known me forever and, perhaps more than anyone else, could understand where I was coming from.

We planned a day trip—ride bikes, ferry to Toronto Island Park, have a picnic—and decided that every time we noticed anything less than perfect in ourselves, in others, or in the world, we would celebrate it. We called this game "celebrating imperfection."

It didn't take long for the celebration to begin. While queuing up my bike for the ferry I brushed against the chain and got ugly black grease on my pants. I pointed it out to my friend and shouted, "Woo-hoo!" On the island, we spread out our picnic blanket and realized she had forgotten to pack a knife to cut the cheese. "Hurray!" we cheered. We did a little victory dance on the blanket and spread chunks of soft cheese on our bread with our fingers. We both wanted to go for a swim, but we'd forgotten to pack our bathing suits, so we gave each other high fives, stripped down to our underwear, and jumped into the water. Together we celebrated our imperfect day.

So many things go wrong in our lives every day that it feels natural to complain and blame. What would it feel like to treat imperfection as something to celebrate? Turn to the next and final exercise to find out.

Celebrate Imperfection

Today you will turn everything that doesn't go the way you'd like into a cause for celebration. This includes all the mistakes that you, or others, make, as well as anything that disappoints or embarrasses you. If you're having a bad hair day, shout, "Yay!" If traffic lights turn red right before you get to them, pump your fists in the air and say, "Woo-hoo!" If you drop your coffee cup as you're putting the lid on, dance a little jig, being careful not to slip on the puddle on the floor.

On any given day things will not go perfectly. The traffic, the weather, and our computers may not behave as we would like. We're likely to goof up at some point; our kids, friends, and coworkers will too. While imperfect performance is the natural order of life, as perfectionists we unconsciously hold the monkey mind-set of *If I make a mistake, forget something, or things don't go as planned, everything will be ruined.* The mantra of the monkey is safety and predictability, and when things go off script, the monkey throws a fit. And we usually respond by tightening our bodies, judging ourselves and others, and complaining, all behaviors that feed the little critter.

We cannot change the natural order of life, but we can certainly change how we respond to it! By choosing to celebrate imperfection, we are redirecting ourselves to a new expansive mind-set: *When I make a mistake, forget something, or things don't go as planned, it is an opportunity to exercise control over the only thing I can control—my response.* This strategy will build resilience, enabling us to recover more quickly from mistakes and mishaps. And by choosing to bring humor and a lighthearted playfulness to less-than-perfect moments, we foster more spontaneity and joy throughout the whole of our life.

Our limbic system makes sure that it feels painful when things go wrong, especially when we are at fault. Disappointment, blame, and shame are just a few of the emotions that may arise. But as Buddhists teach, pain is inevitable; suffering is optional. What they mean is that when we resist pain by tensing up, complaining, and judging ourselves and others, we create suffering. So, today, open up and welcome your pain. Celebrate it, not only in your mind but using your breath, your entire body.

Don't grade yourself too harshly today. Our default response to frustrating imperfection—tightening up and getting upset—can happen so fast that you may not catch yourself in time to stop it. That's okay. After you groan, swear, or call yourself names, gently remind yourself that today you are celebrating mishaps, and then shout, "Yippee!" It may sound artificial or forced, but no matter; better late than never. Any time you redirect yourself to your expansive mind-set and welcome uncomfortable emotions, you are getting a workout— and moving toward your true values. That's something to celebrate!

Epilogue

Congratulations for your willingness to embrace this workout! I encourage you to retake the Perfectionism Quiz available for download at http://monkeymindbooks.com/p/. I'm betting you'll notice a change in your quiz score that parallels a change in your life.

To recap, here are the qualities you've been nurturing doing these exercises:

Tolerance of criticism, enabling you to incorporate feedback that will help you grow

Willingness to make mistakes, allowing you to use trial and error to progress

Ability to stop working even when tasks are unfinished, freeing yourself for self-care and quality time with family and friends

Immunity to others' judgments, so you can be honest, authentic, and vulnerable

Courage to risk failure, so you can pursue the difficult goals that will bring you the greatest fulfillment

Ability to delegate, which empowers you to harness the power of others and free yourself from burnout

Like a physical workout, you need to maintain this psychological workout for it to be effective. To keep and build on the gains you've made with these thirty exercises, make them part of your daily routine. How much freedom from perfectionism do you want? Ultimately, there's no limit to the spontaneity, creativity, authenticity, self-care, connection, purpose, and self-compassion you can enjoy. So tomorrow, and every day thereafter, *don't forget your daily sweat!*

Jennifer Shannon, LMFT, is author of *Don't Feed the Monkey Mind, The Shyness and Social Anxiety Workbook for Teens, The Anxiety Survival Guide for Teens,* and *A Teen's Guide to Getting Stuff Done.* She is a diplomate of the Academy of Cognitive Therapy.

Illustrator **Doug Shannon** is a freelance cartoonist.

ABOUT US

Founded by psychologist Matthew McKay and Patrick Fanning, New Harbinger has published books that promote wellness in mind, body, and spirit for more than forty-five years.

Our proven-effective self-help books and pioneering workbooks help readers of all ages and backgrounds make positive lifestyle changes, improve mental health and well-being, and achieve meaningful personal growth. In addition, our spirituality books offer profound guidance for deepening awareness and cultivating healing, self-discovery, and fulfillment.

New Harbinger is proud to be an independent and employee-owned company, publishing books that reflect its core values of integrity, innovation, commitment, sustainability, compassion, and trust. Written by leaders in the field and recommended by therapists worldwide, New Harbinger books are practical, reliable, and provide real tools for real change.

MORE WAYS to OVERCOME
A MONKEY MINDSET!

A cognitive behavioral therapy (CBT)-based approach to help you stop feeding your anxious thoughts and find the peace you crave.

ISBN: 978-1626255067 / US $17.95

This fun, illustrated guide offers a 30-day anxiety-busting workout for building calm and increasing confidence.

ISBN: 978-1684035885 / US $16.95

new**harbinger**publications

1-800-748-6273 / newharbinger.com